Author: Jed Dolton
Publisher: Daoudi Publishing
ISBN: 978-1960809070

Introduction

Welcome to our decodable book for struggling readers in grade 1! This book is designed to help children who are having difficulty sounding out words and confusing similar letters such as b, d, p, and q. It also focuses on letters with similar sounds such as d, t, b, p, f, and v. We understand that signs of dyslexia can present differently depending on the age range, and that's why this workbook is specifically tailored to meet the needs of struggling readers in grade 1.

Our book includes eight activity packets for each letter, where children will engage in fun activities such as reading and tracing the letter, tracing and writing simple sentences, finding the missing sound, circling the sound, finding the correct words, tracing, writing, and coloring the comic letters, marking the appropriate box to show where the letter is in the word (beginning, middle, or end), and a bonus reading list of 44 decodable words.

We believe that learning should be enjoyable and engaging, and that's why we've included various phonics games, word associations, matching, coloring, and more in our book. Cheerful illustrations and coloring comic alphabets will make it easier for kids to remember sight words rather than just memorizing them, which can be a powerful tool when reading.

Whether your child is in preschool or grade school, a struggling reader, reluctant, or simply needs a little push in the right direction, you will find this book helpful. So, let's get started and help your child unlock the joy of reading!

This Book
Belong to

_____

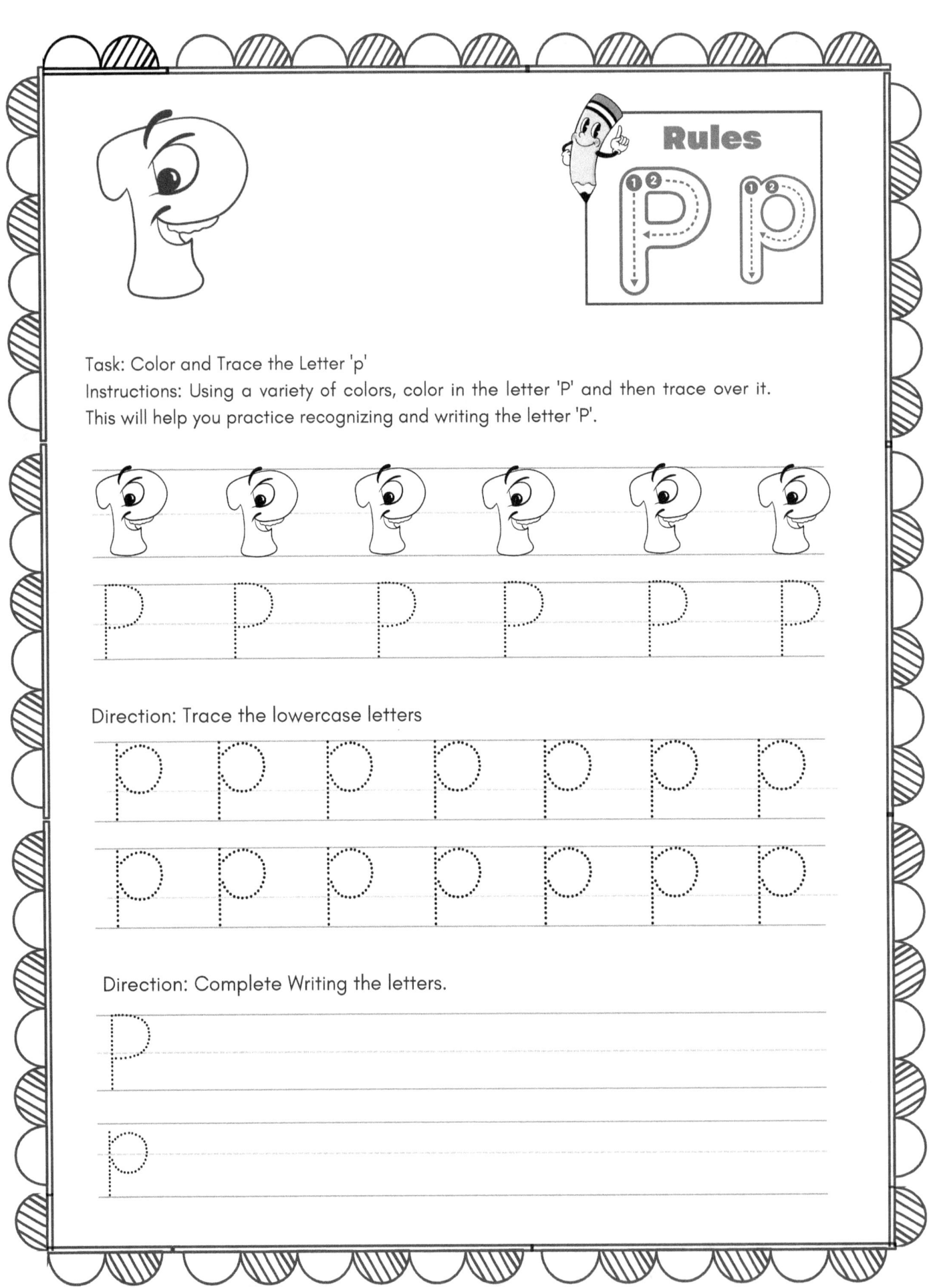

Rules

Task: Color and Trace the Letter 'p'

Instructions: Using a variety of colors, color in the letter 'P' and then trace over it. This will help you practice recognizing and writing the letter 'P'.

Direction: Trace the lowercase letters

Direction: Complete Writing the letters.

First, trace the sentence.
Then write it on your own.

I have a pen

I see a big hippo

I love the pool

Pin in pot

Piece of pizza

Rules
1 - Choose the correct word
2 - Circle it
4 - Write below the whole word with missing letter
5 - Mark the wrong word

p 🐷 g
pig

b 🥧 t

m 🐟 L

d 🐙 m

s h i 🚢

📷 a n

a p 🍎 l e

m 🚗 p

s l e e 🛏️

b ✉️ w

🐾 a w

r 🦁 v

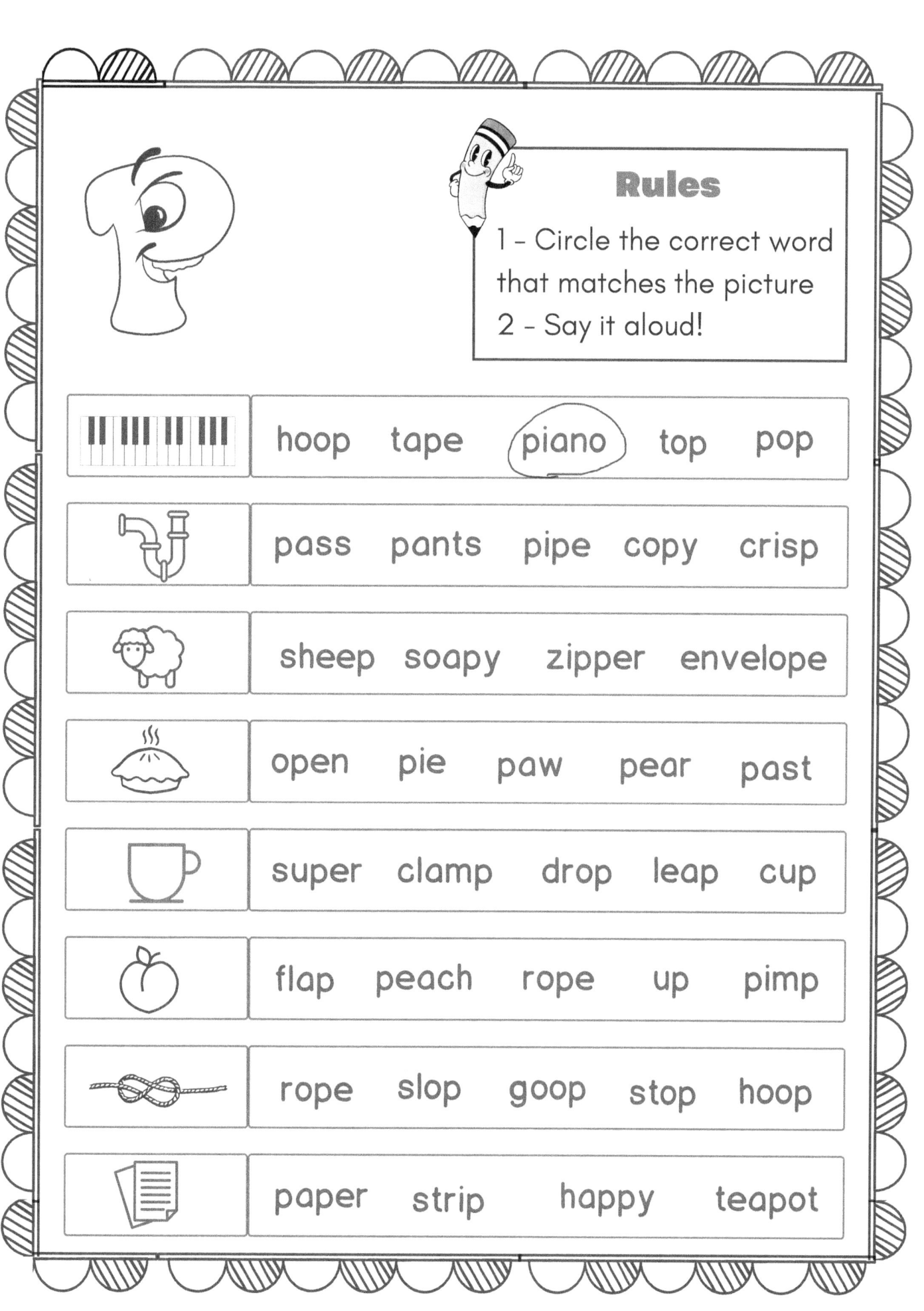

Rules

1 – Circle the correct word that matches the picture
2 – Say it aloud!

	hoop tape (piano) top pop
	pass pants pipe copy crisp
	sheep soapy zipper envelope
	open pie paw pear past
	super clamp drop leap cup
	flap peach rope up pimp
	rope slop goop stop hoop
	paper strip happy teapot

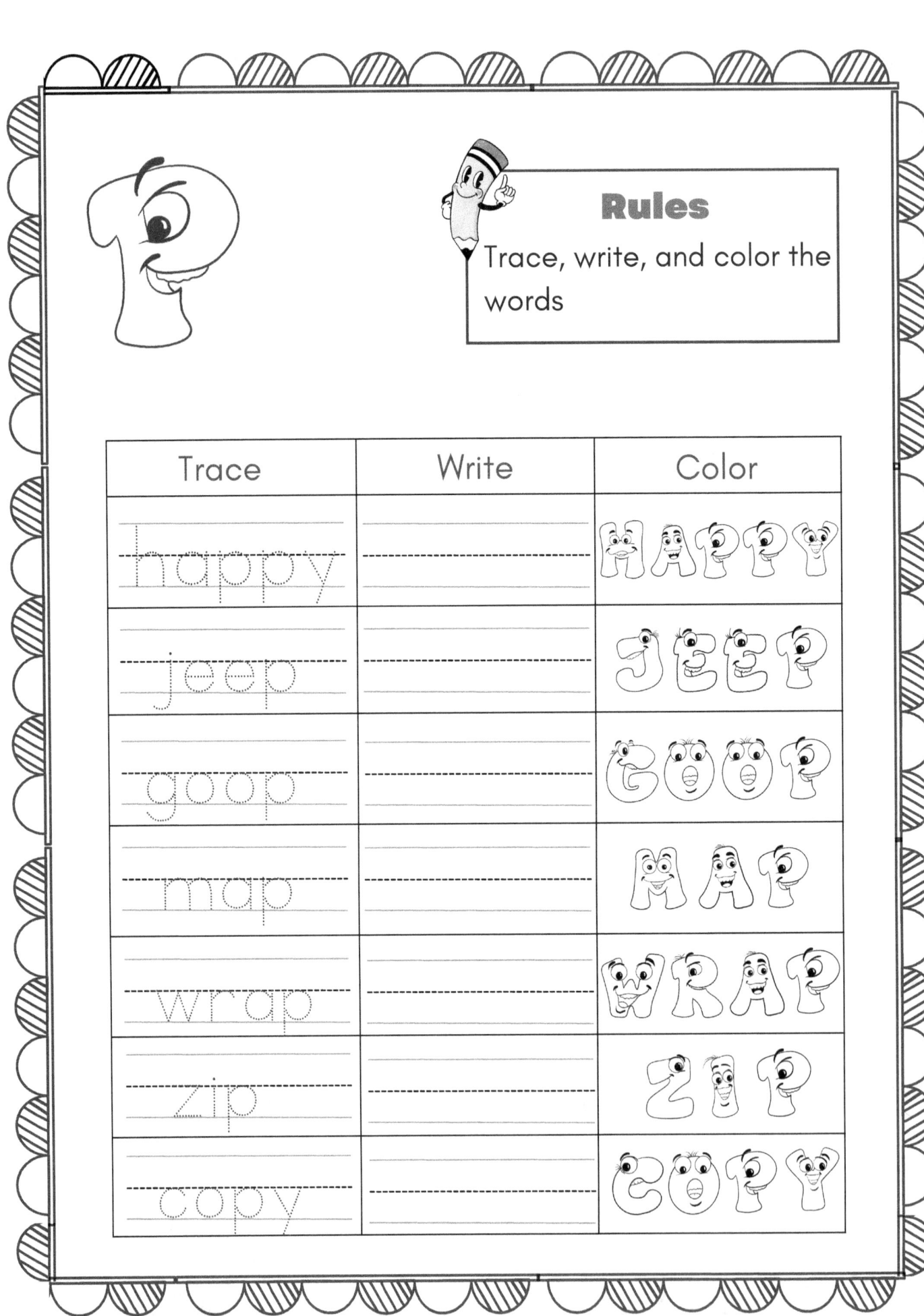

Rules
Trace, write, and color the words

Trace	Write	Color
happy		HAPPY
jeep		JEEP
goop		GOOP
map		MAP
wrap		WRAP
zip		ZIP
copy		COPY

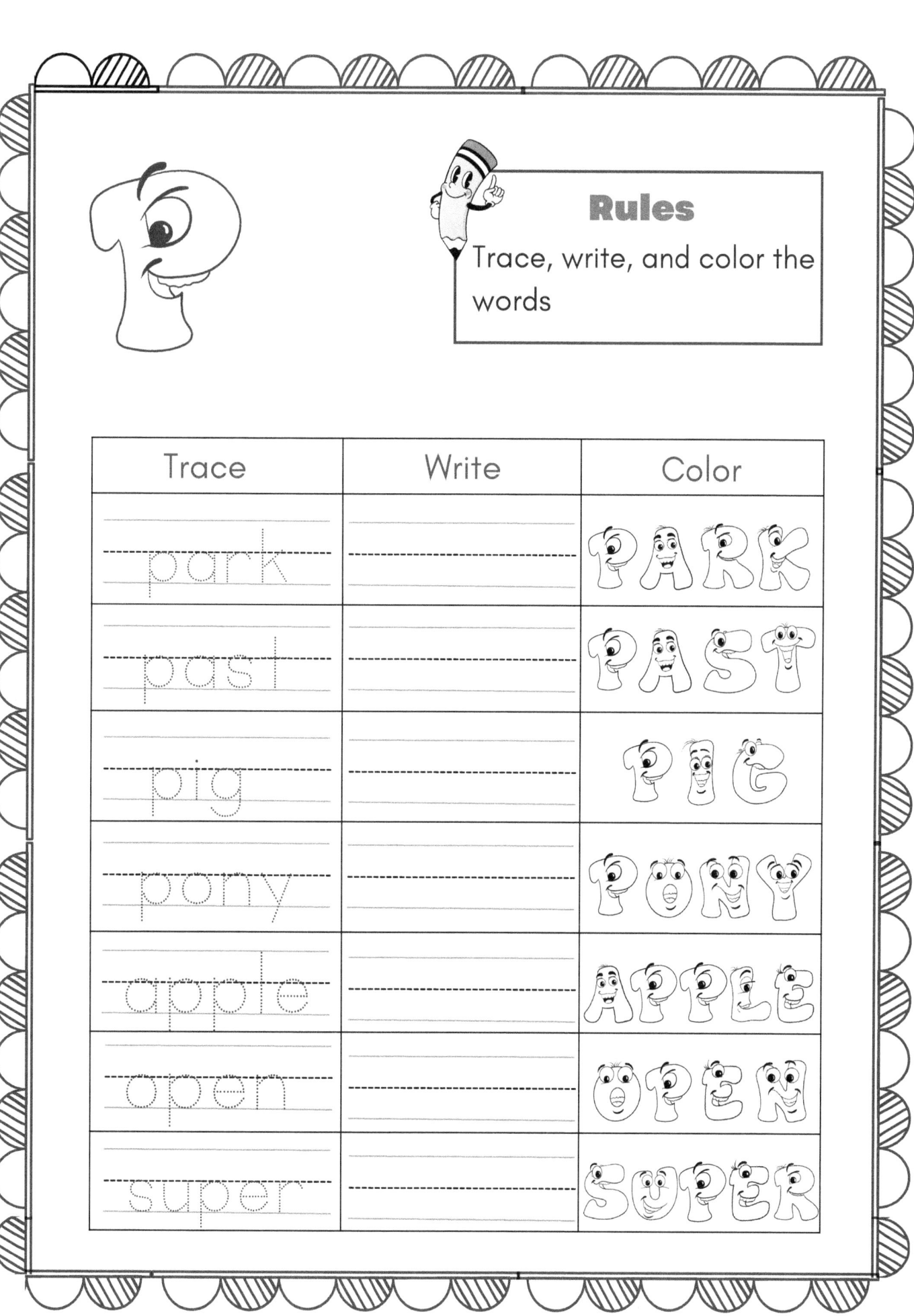

Rules

Trace, write, and color the words

Trace	Write	Color
park		PARK
past		PAST
pig		PIG
pony		PONY
apple		APPLE
open		OPEN
super		SUPER

Rules

Read each word and then mark the appropriate box indicating where the letter 'p' is located in the word – at the beginning, middle, or end

Word	Beginning	Middle	End
pencil	X		
splat		X	
sleep			X
strap			
palm			
sump			
pot			
tape			
hippo			
pick			
top			
split			

Reading list

Read every word aloud!

lamp	pat	yelp	flop
pet	pit	pot	swap
skip	pop	deep	romp
tip	pen	dip	pick
seep	pile	gulp	reap
map	clip	park	pear
pack	peck	pump	pink
spider	open	play	hoop
pot	soap	slop	apple
pap	palm	pond	nip
split	diaper	piano	dup

Rules

Task: Color and Trace the Letter 'B'
Instructions: Using a variety of colors, color in the letter 'B' and then trace over it.
This will help you practice recognizing and writing the letter 'B'.

Direction: Trace the lowercase letters

Direction: Complete writing the letters.

Rules

First, trace the sentence.
Then write it on your own.

Flying bird high
Flying

Brown cow jumps

Bread is yummy

Big brown dog

Teddy on bed

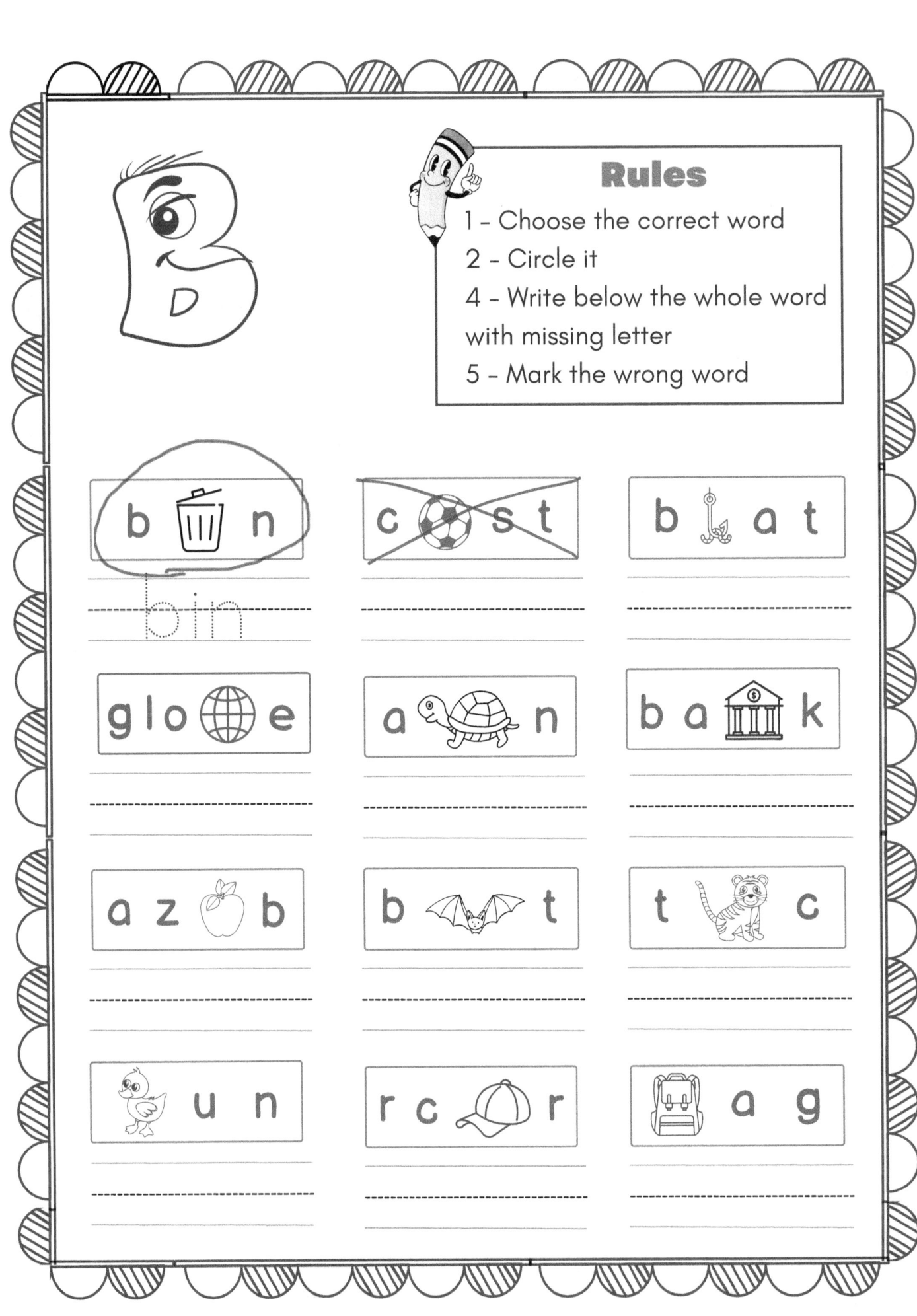

Rules

1 – Choose the correct word
2 – Circle it
4 – Write below the whole word with missing letter
5 – Mark the wrong word

b 🗑 n

bin

c ⚽ s t

b 🪝 a t

g l o 🌐 e

a 🐢 n

b a 🏦 k

a z 🍎 b

b 🦇 t

t 🐯 c

🐤 u n

r c 🧢 r

🎒 a g

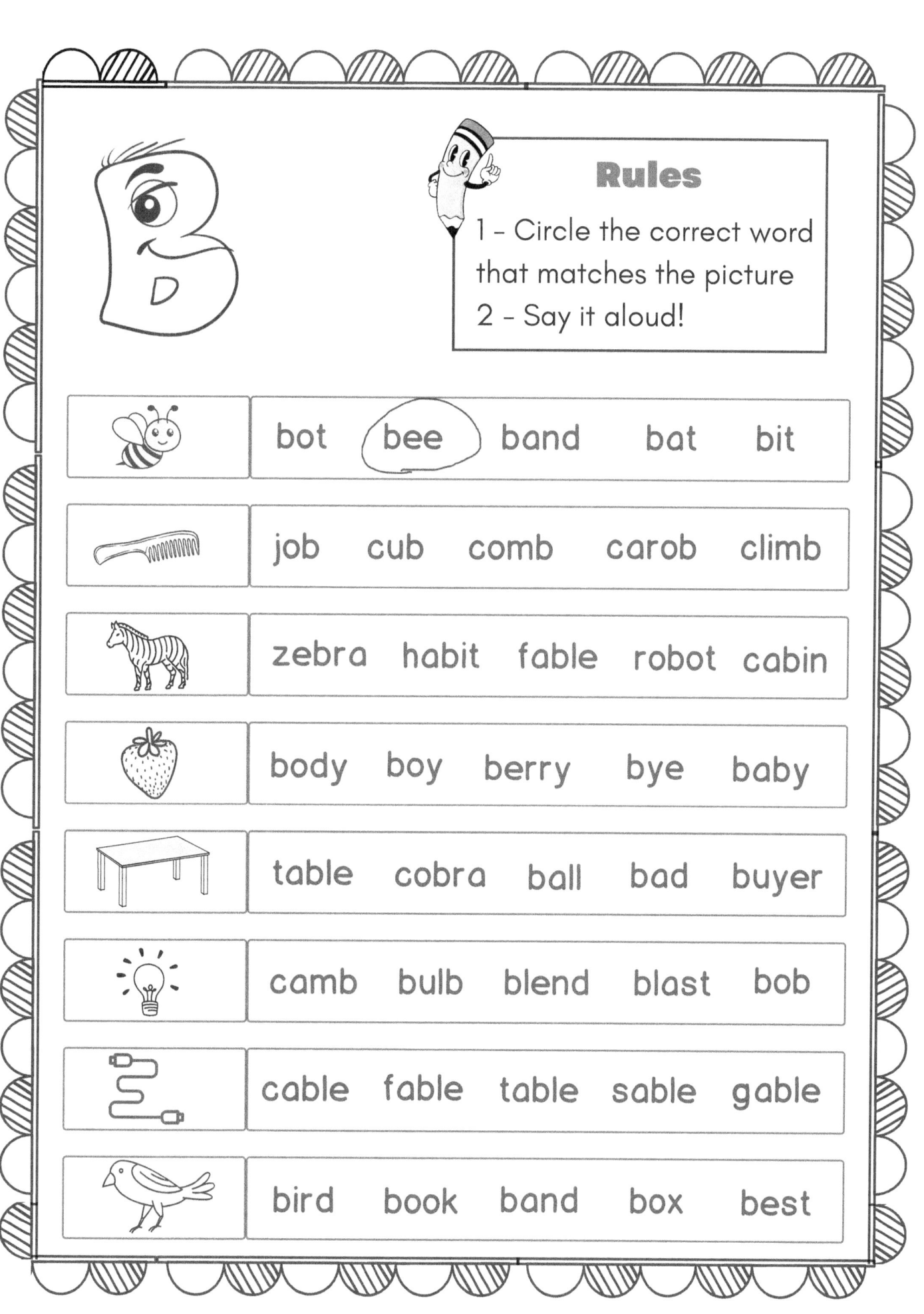

Rules

1 – Circle the correct word that matches the picture
2 – Say it aloud!

	bot （bee） band bat bit
	job cub comb carob climb
	zebra habit fable robot cabin
	body boy berry bye baby
	table cobra ball bad buyer
	camb bulb blend blast bob
	cable fable table sable gable
	bird book band box best

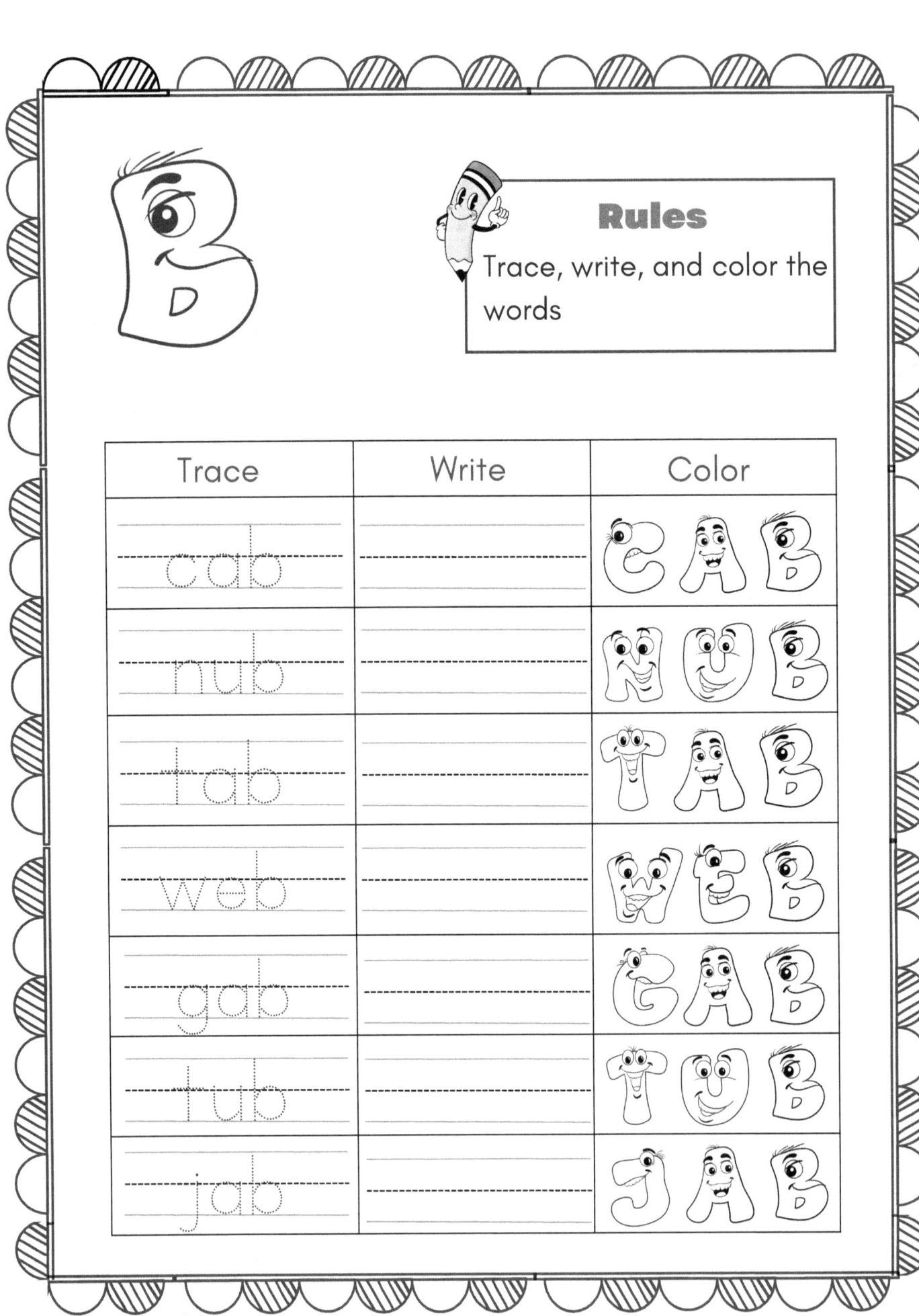

Rules

Trace, write, and color the words

Trace	Write	Color
cab		CAB
nub		NUB
tab		TAB
web		WEB
gab		GAB
tub		TUB
jab		JAB

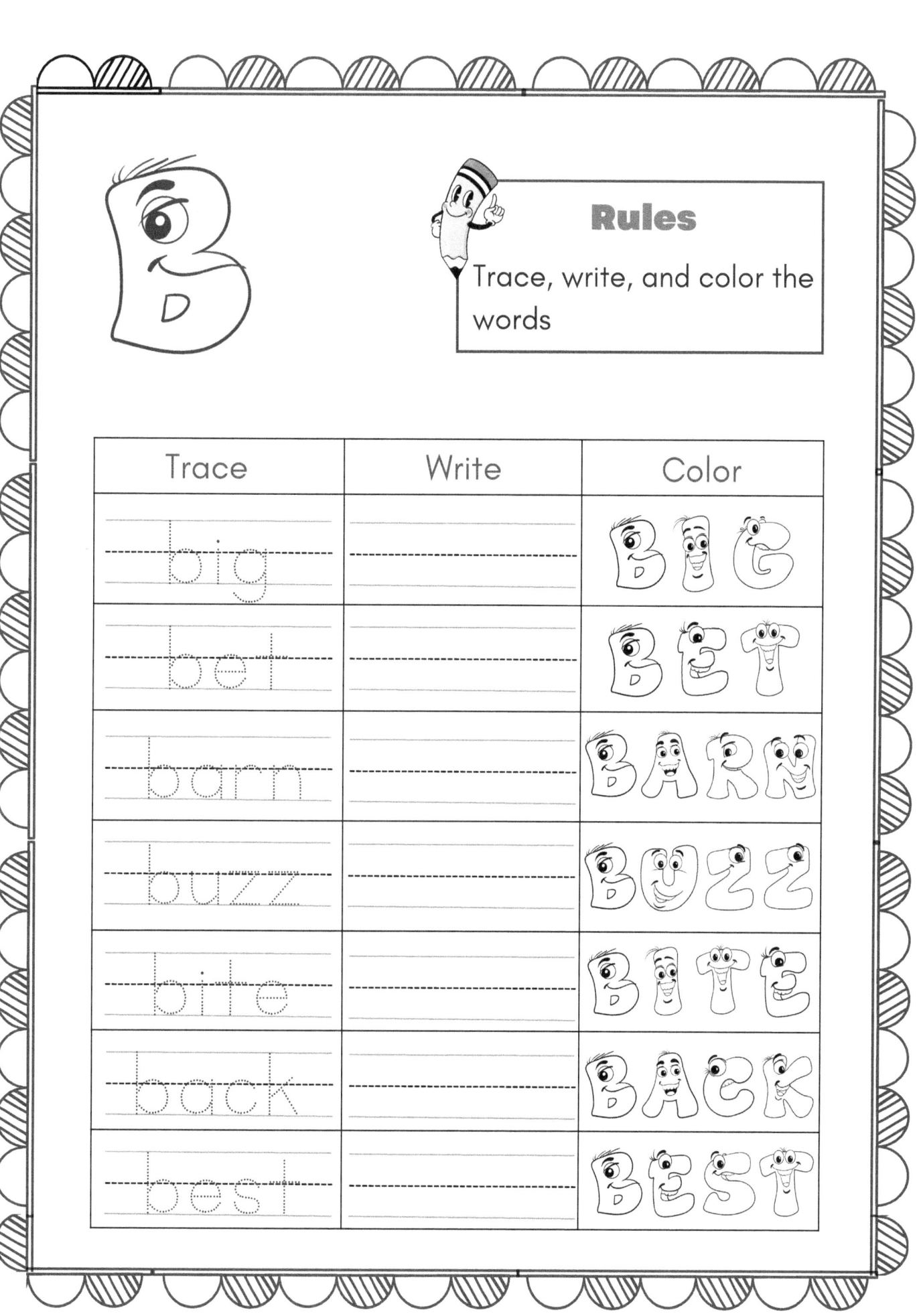

Rules

Trace, write, and color the words

Trace	Write	Color
big		BIG
bet		BET
barn		BARN
buzz		BUZZ
bite		BITE
back		BACK
best		BEST

Rules

Read each word and then mark the appropriate box indicating where the letter 'b' is located in the word – at the beginning, middle, or end

Word	Beginning	Middle	End
habit		X	
crib			X
bid	X		
ban			
gable			
club			
rubber			
nab			
tabby			
swab			
blab			
bop			

Reading list

Read every word aloud!

bug	bean	bird	boo
rib	bus	sub	rub
web	bud	bee	ball
ban	bop	hub	crib
job	bill	bog	blob
bed	tube	sob	rib
nab	blab	lab	bib
busy	bat	bin	mob
job	dab	rob	sob
cab	rub	cub	box
bag	bow	boy	bib

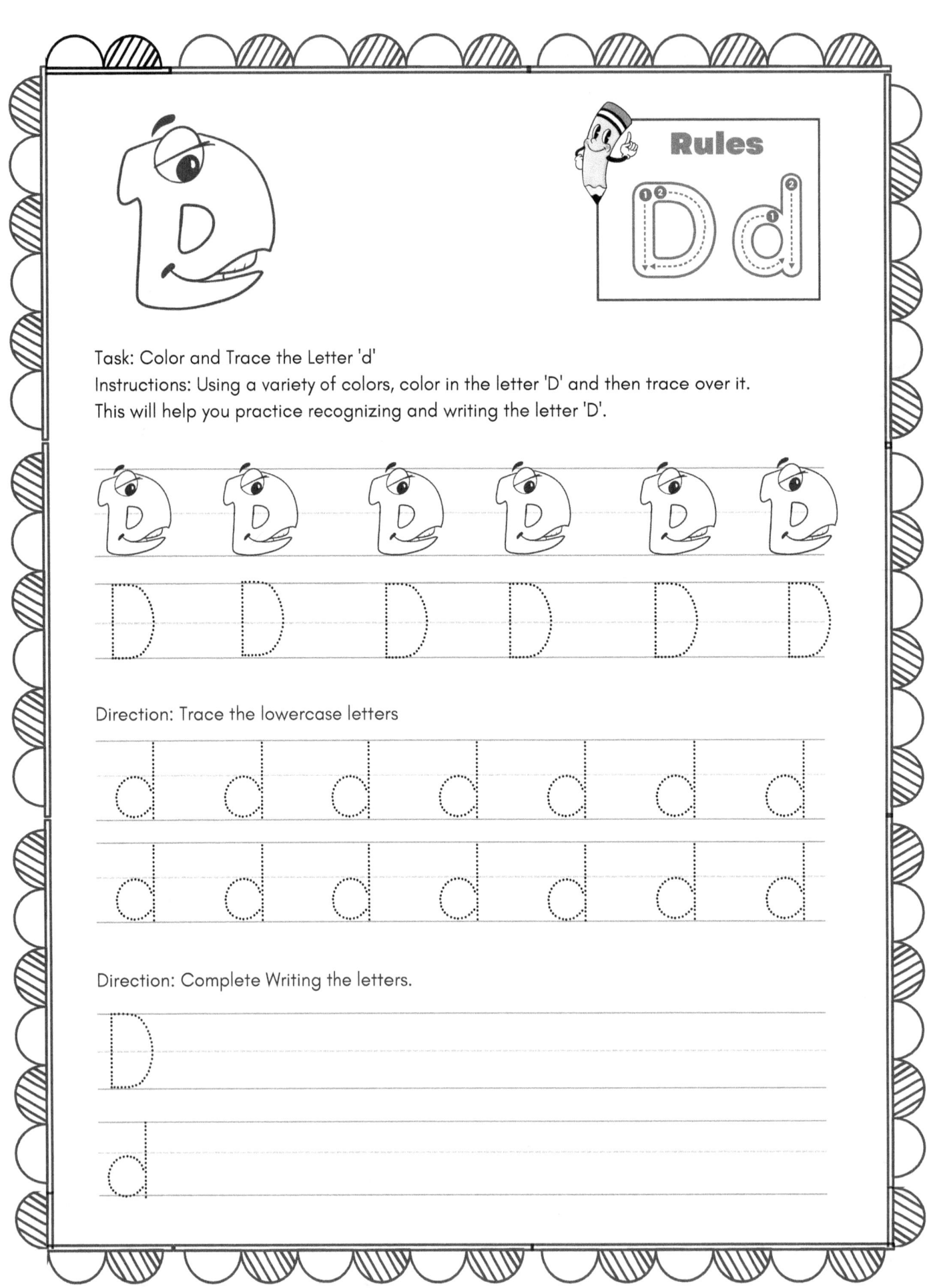

Rules

Task: Color and Trace the Letter 'd'

Instructions: Using a variety of colors, color in the letter 'D' and then trace over it.
This will help you practice recognizing and writing the letter 'D'.

Direction: Trace the lowercase letters

Direction: Complete Writing the letters.

Rules

First, trace the sentence.
Then write it on your own.

Big dinosaur

Big

I play drums

Wooden door

Riding the horse

I love ducks

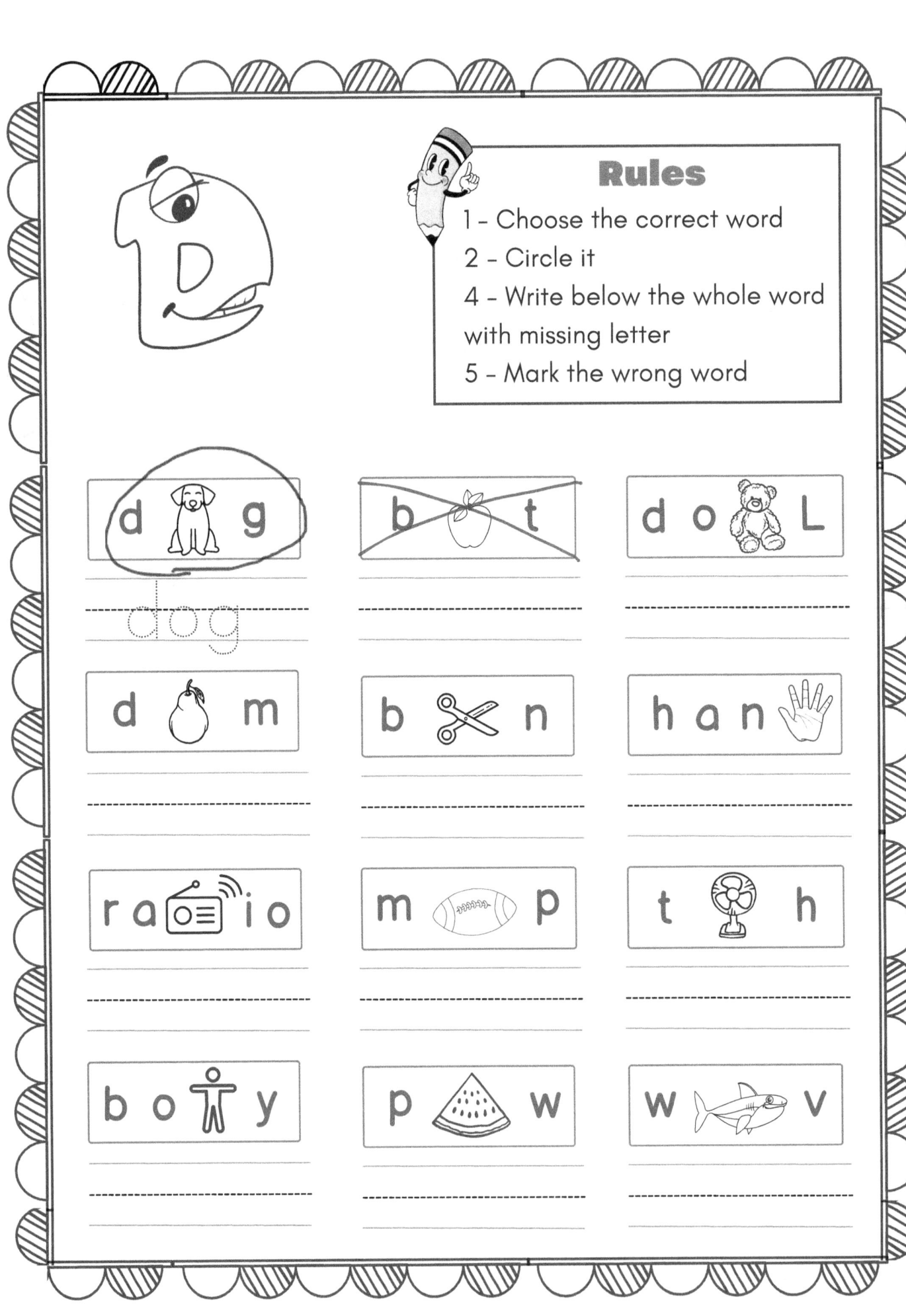

Rules

1 - Choose the correct word
2 - Circle it
4 - Write below the whole word with missing letter
5 - Mark the wrong word

d 🐕 g

d o g

b 🍎 t

d o L

d 🍐 m

b ✂ n

h a n ✋

r a 📻 i o

m 🏈 p

t 🌀 h

b o 🧍 y

p 🍉 w

w 🦈 v

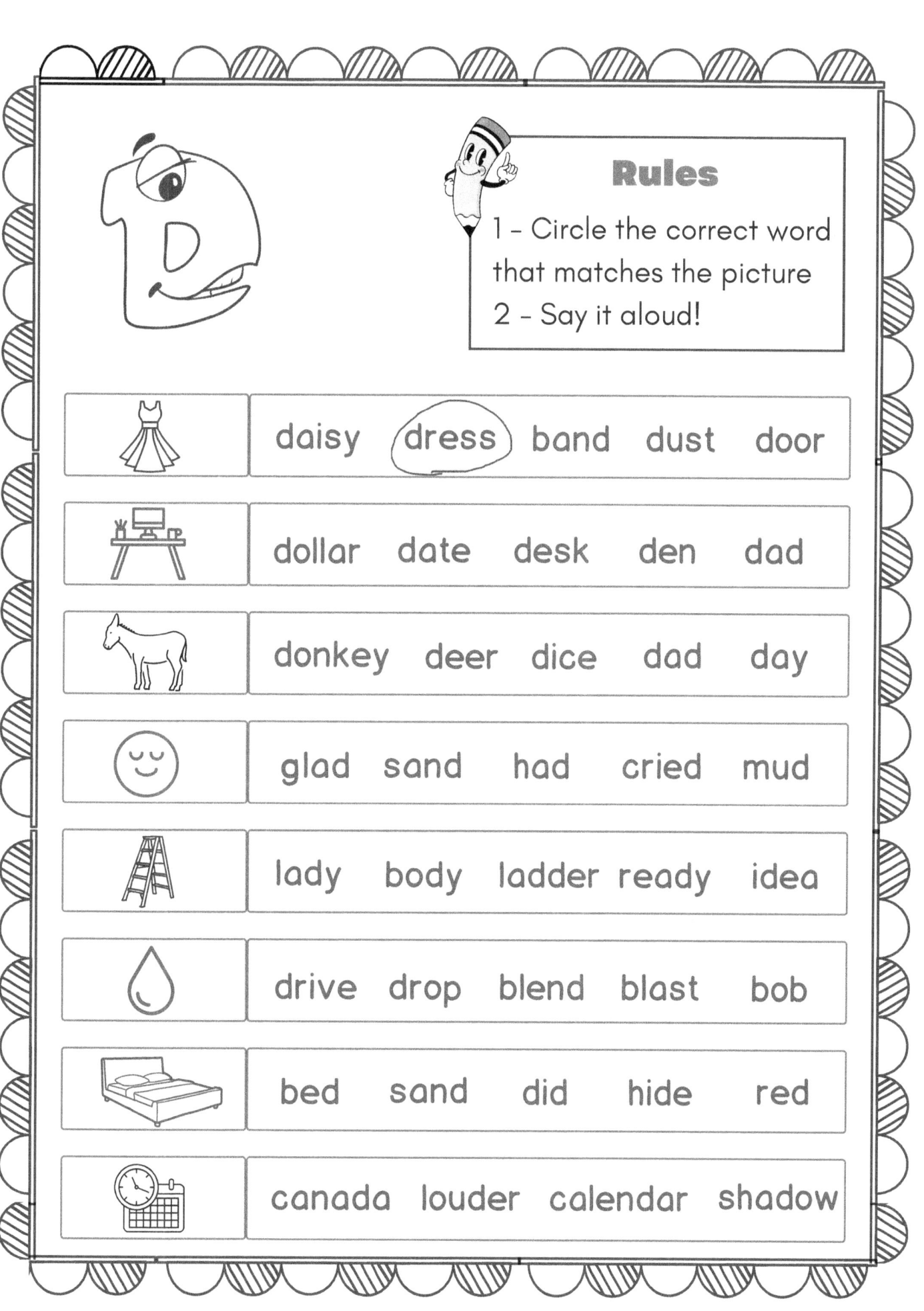

daisy (dress) band dust door

dollar date desk den dad

donkey deer dice dad day

glad sand had cried mud

lady body ladder ready idea

drive drop blend blast bob

bed sand did hide red

canada louder calendar shadow

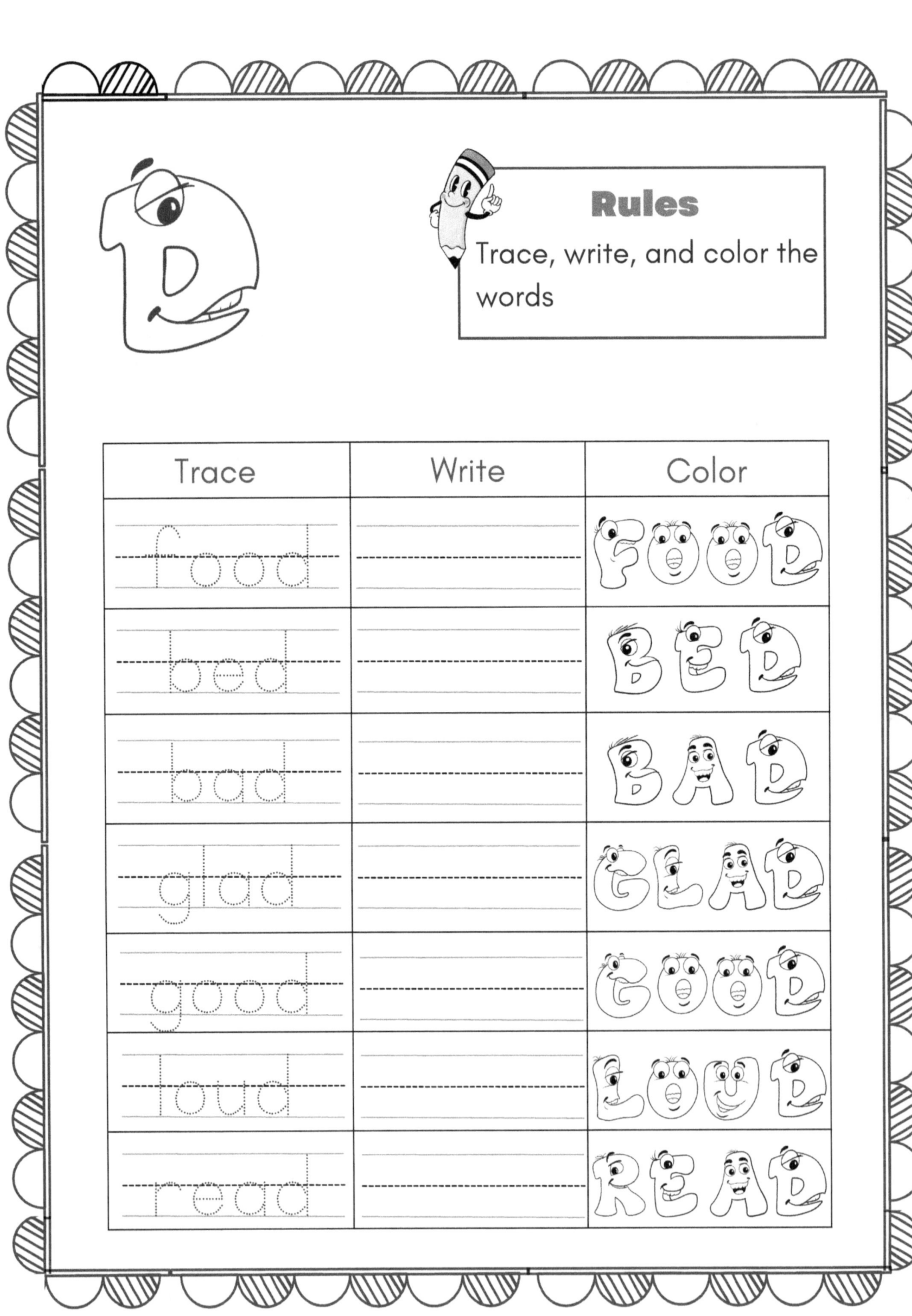

Rules

Trace, write, and color the words

Trace	Write	Color
food		FOOD
bed		BED
bad		BAD
glad		GLAD
good		GOOD
loud		LOUD
read		READ

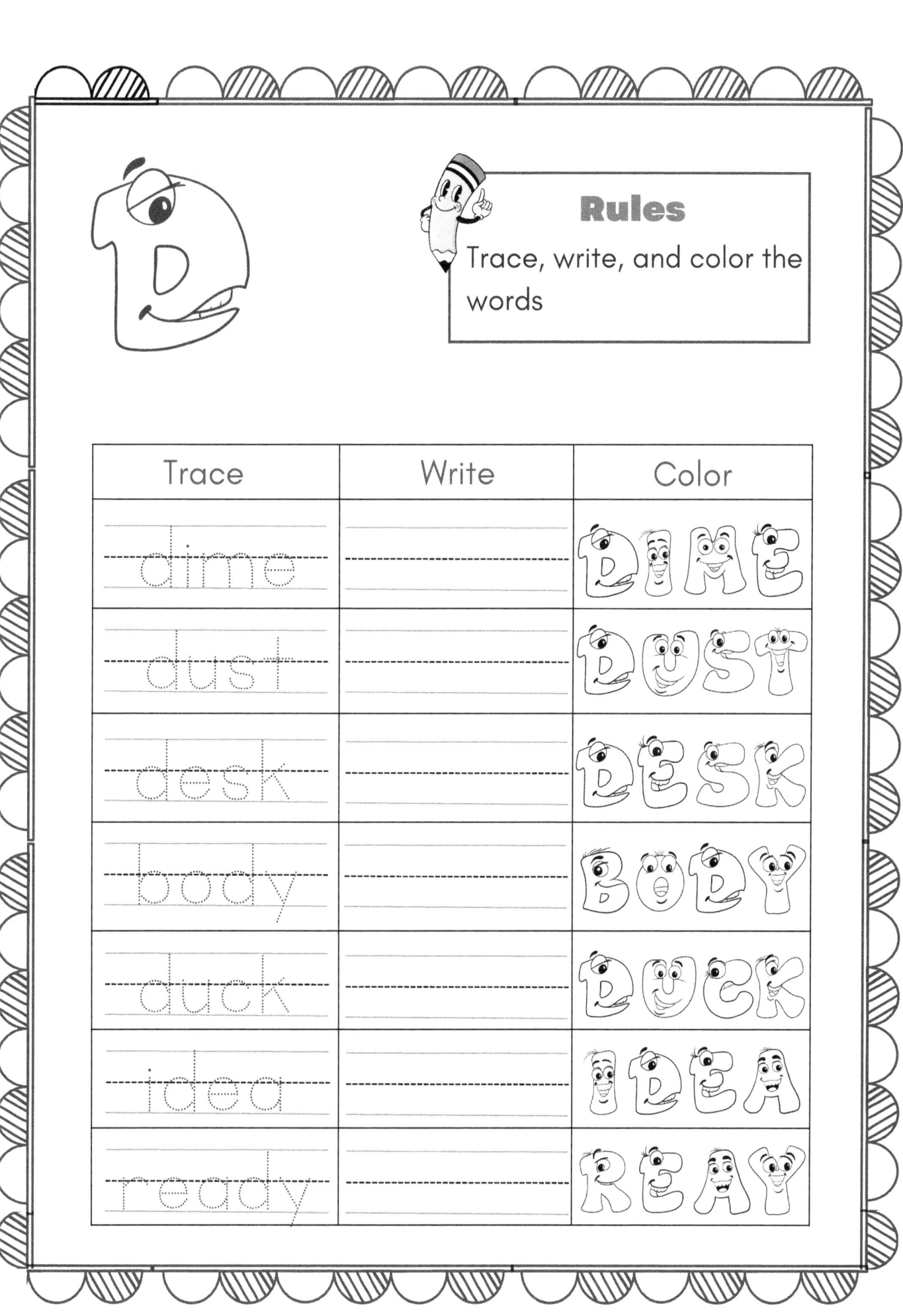

Rules

Trace, write, and color the words

Trace	Write	Color
dime		DIME
dust		DUST
desk		DESK
body		BODY
duck		DUCK
idea		IDEA
ready		REAY

Rules

Read each word and then mark the appropriate box indicating where the letter 'd' is located in the word – at the beginning, middle, or end

Word	Beginning	Middle	End
dice	X		
red			X
comedy		X	
food			
dart			
dent			
dull			
badge			
fad			
dot			
wed			
bedtime			

Reading list

Read every word aloud!

dog	food	bird	date
daily	deem	dinosaur	dose
dart	deer	deep	bud
cod	doctor	dip	dab
fad	wed	fad	bid
down	draw	deal	dive
dent	doom	dust	deaf
ad	nod	sad	damp
does	pod	tad	bed
dig	did	red	do
dot	done	die	dull

Rules

Task: Color and Trace the Letter 'q'

Instructions: Using a variety of colors, color in the letter 'Q' and then trace over it.
This will help you practice recognizing and writing the letter 'Q'.

Direction: Trace the lowercase letters

Direction: Complete Writing the letters.

Rules

First, trace the sentence.
Then write it on your own.

I have a question

Beautiful queen

Quality food

The quail bird

He quit smoking

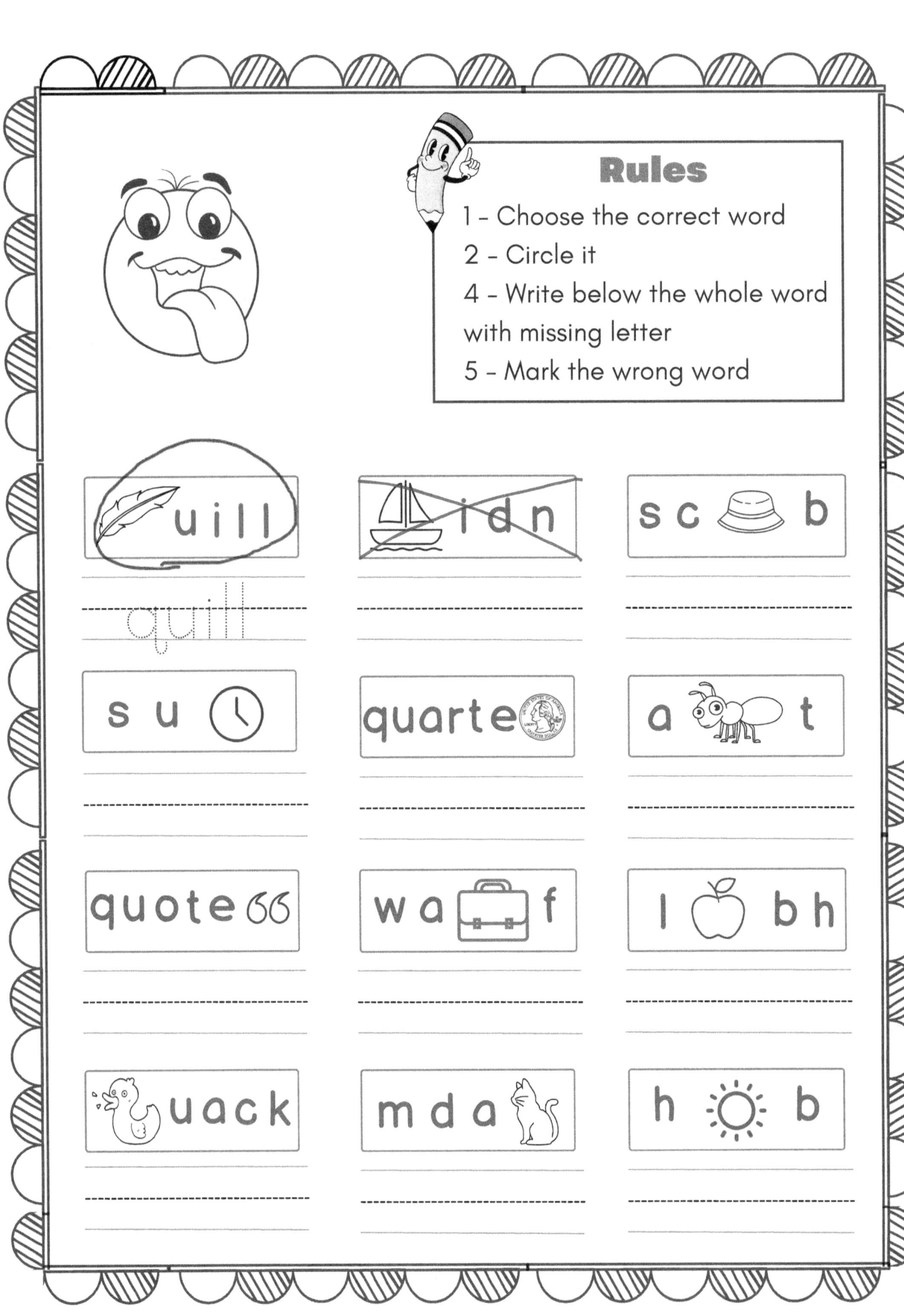

Rules

1 – Choose the correct word
2 – Circle it
4 – Write below the whole word with missing letter
5 – Mark the wrong word

_uill

quill

_idn

sc_b

su_

quarte_

a_t

quote_

wa_f

l_bh

_uack

mda_

h_b

Rules

Read each word and then mark the appropriate box indicating where the letter 'q' is located in the word – at the beginning, middle, or end

Word	Beginning	Middle	End
quake	X		
pique		X	
talaq			X
barque			
quite			
suq			
liquid			
quality			
quid			
quart			
requin			
saq			

Rules

Trace, write, and color the words

Trace	Write	Color
laq		LAQ
squid		SQUID
roq		ROQ
quid		QUID
aqua		AQUA
jeraq		JERAQ
tariq		TARIQ

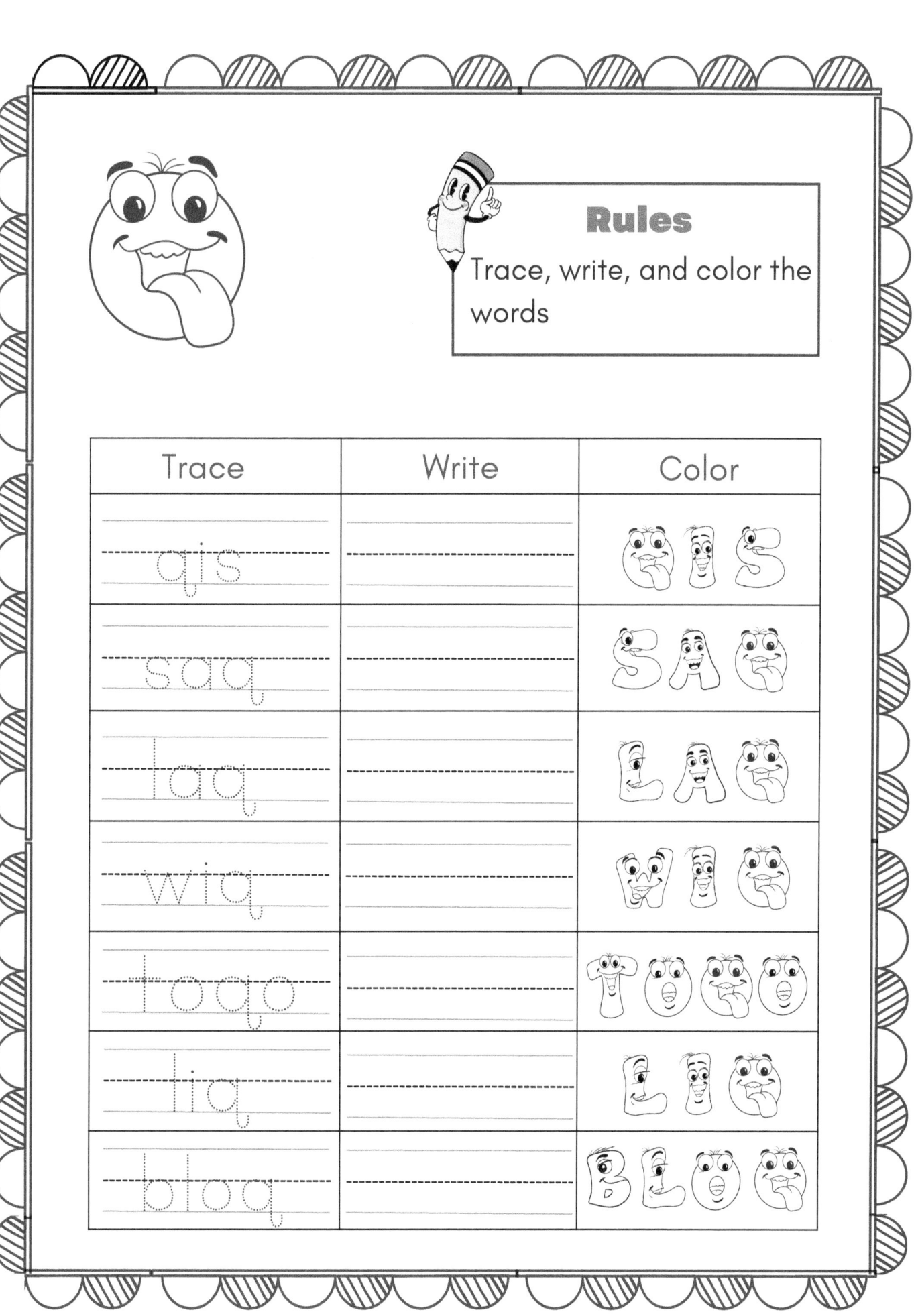

Rules

Trace, write, and color the words

Trace	Write	Color
qis		QIS
saq		SAQ
laq		LAQ
wiq		WIQ
toqo		TOQO
liq		LIQ
bloq		BLOQ

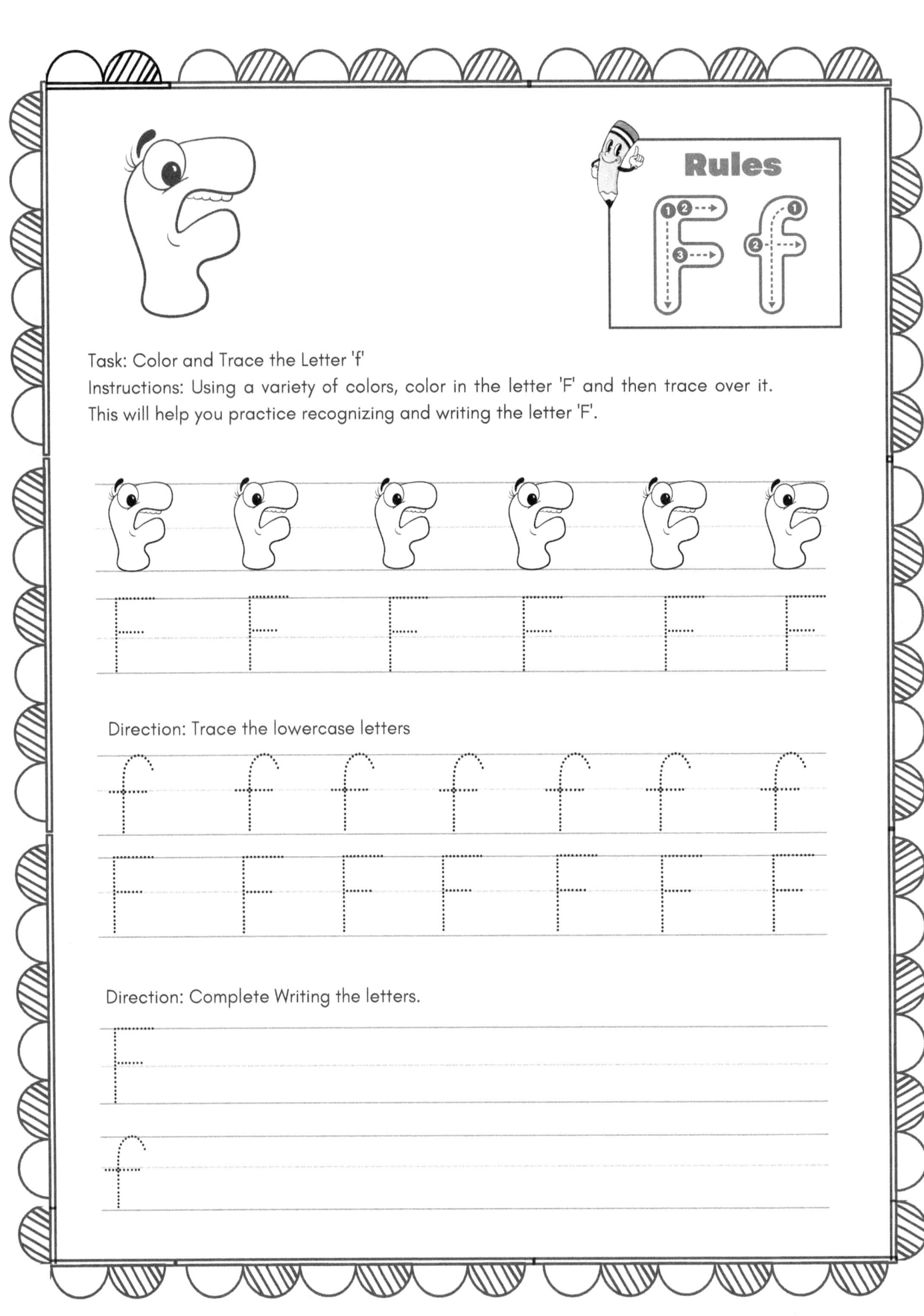

Rules

Task: Color and Trace the Letter 'f'

Instructions: Using a variety of colors, color in the letter 'F' and then trace over it. This will help you practice recognizing and writing the letter 'F'.

Direction: Trace the lowercase letters

Direction: Complete Writing the letters.

Rules

First, trace the sentence.
Then write it on your own.

The horse is fast

The

Fresh coffee

I left my hat

Sly fox

5 I have a five dogs

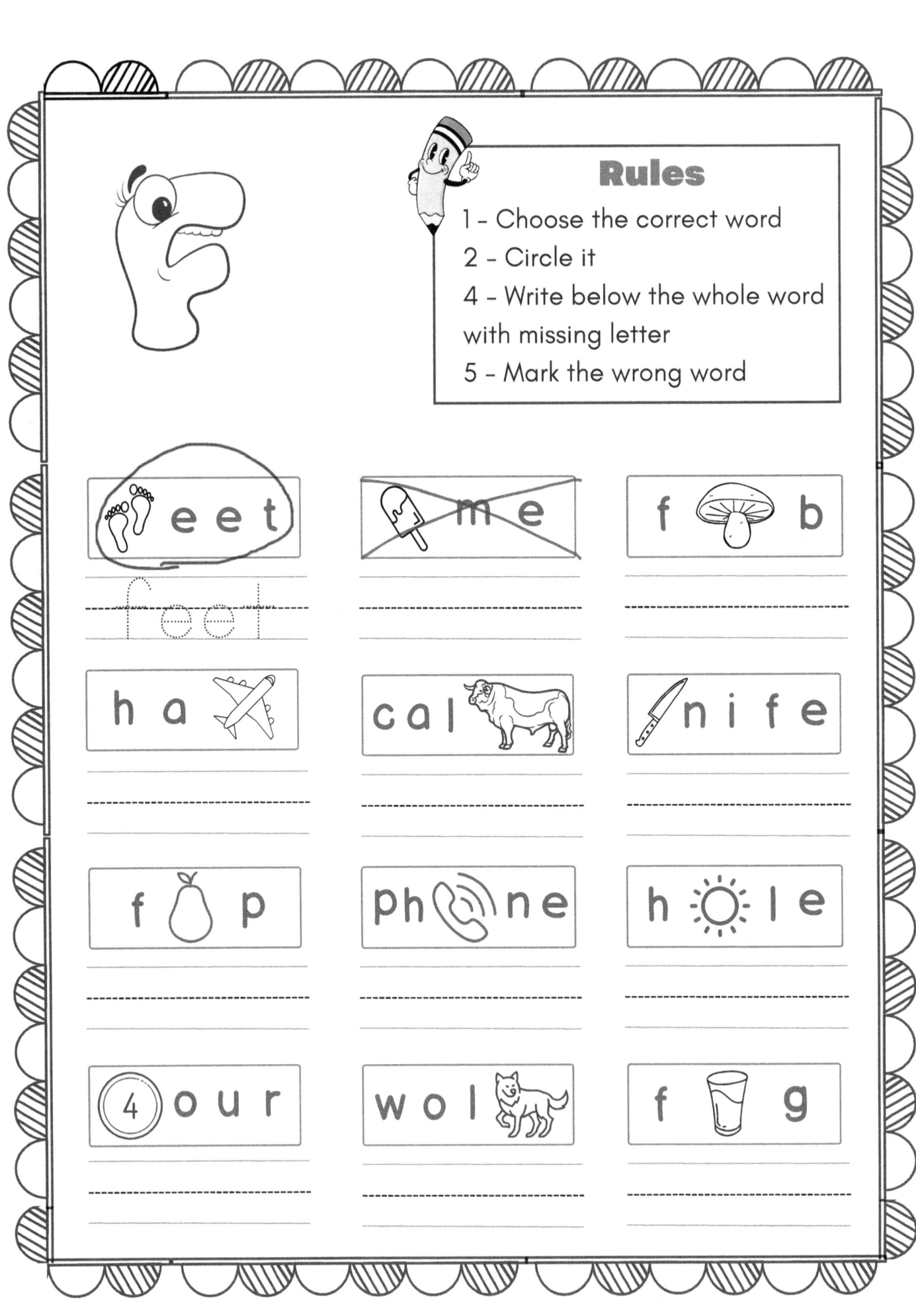

Rules

1 – Choose the correct word
2 – Circle it
4 – Write below the whole word with missing letter
5 – Mark the wrong word

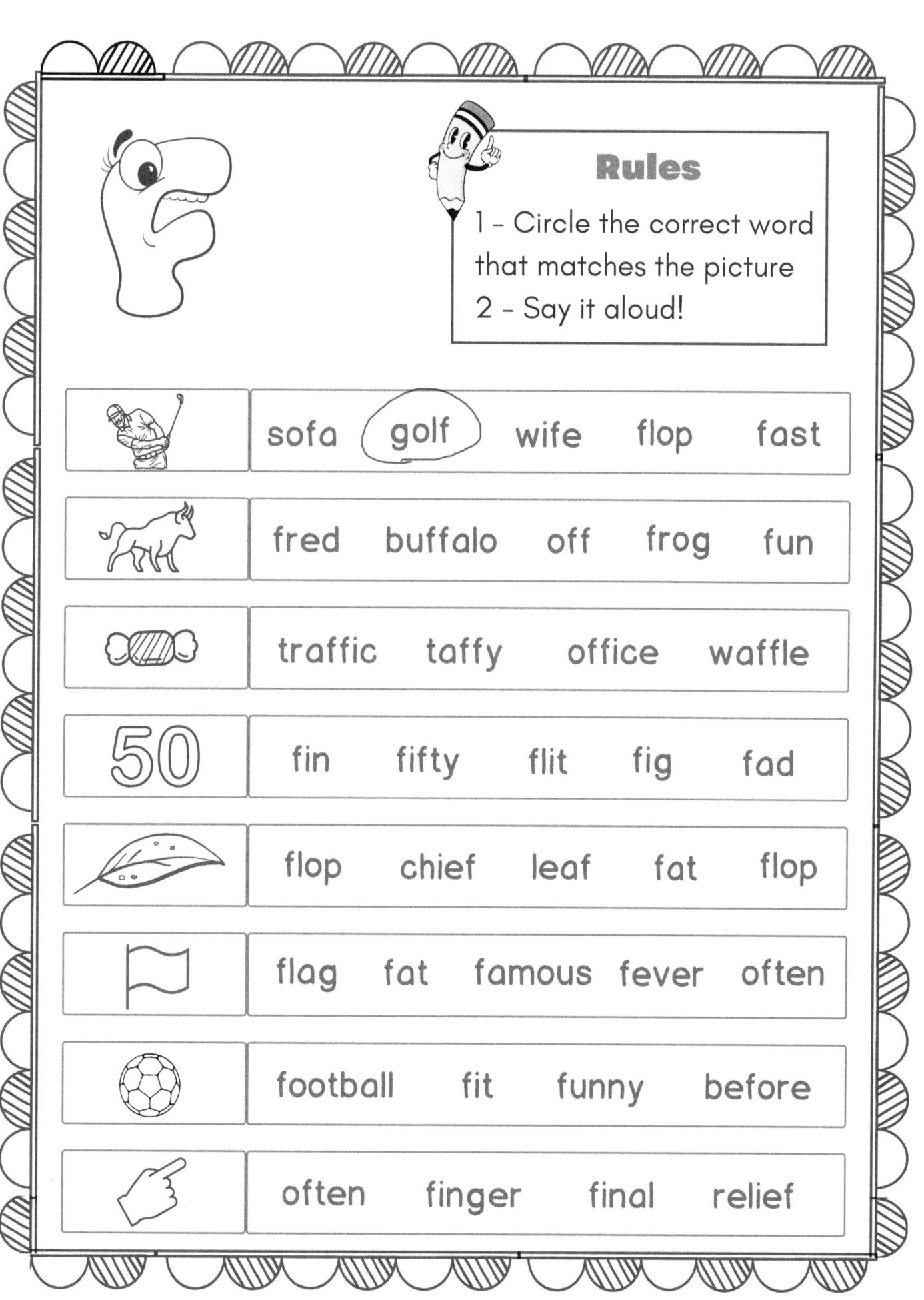

Rules

1 – Circle the correct word that matches the picture
2 – Say it aloud!

	sofa (golf) wife flop fast
	fred buffalo off frog fun
	traffic taffy office waffle
50	fin fifty flit fig fad
	flop chief leaf fat flop
	flag fat famous fever often
	football fit funny before
	often finger final relief

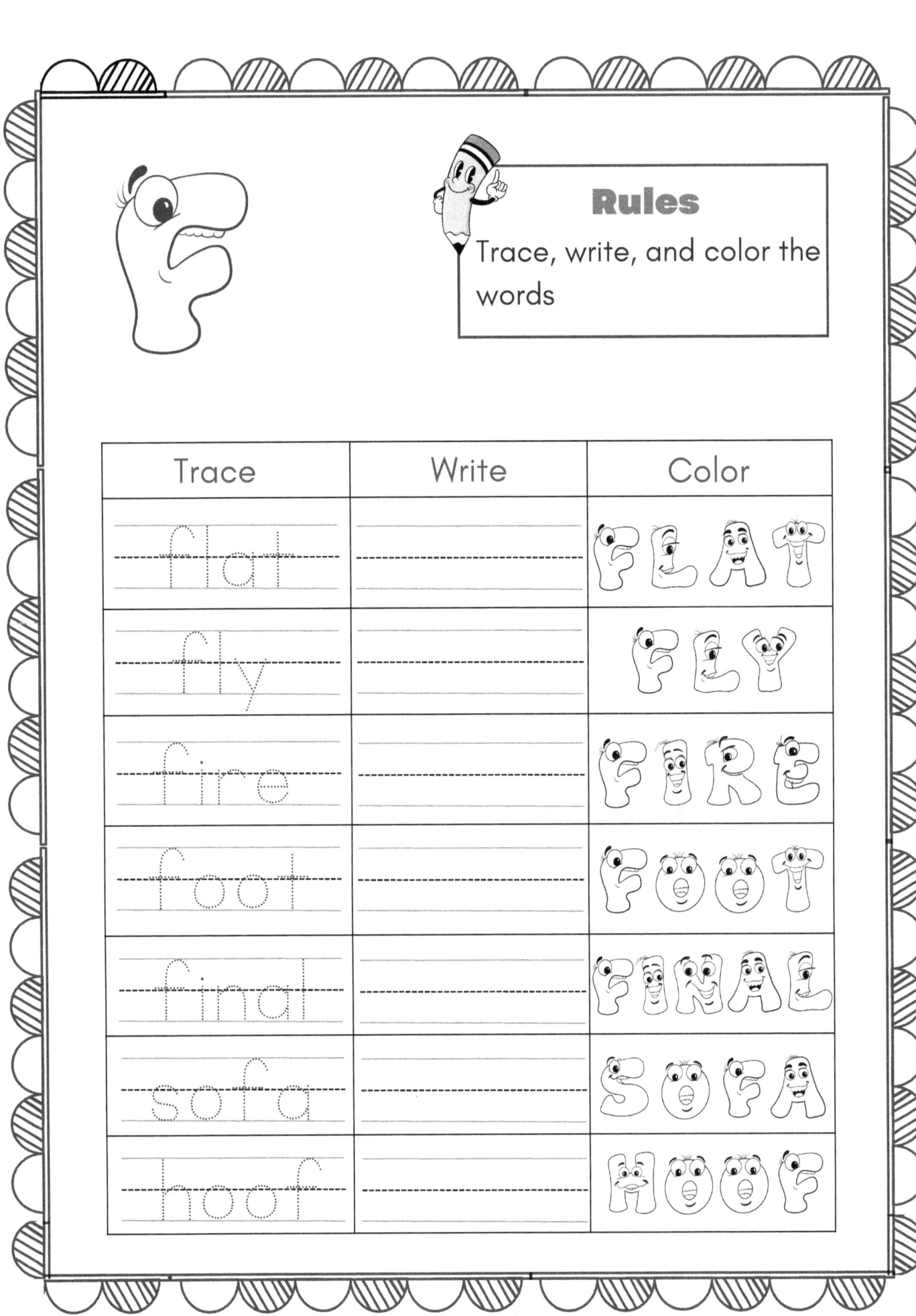

Rules

Trace, write, and color the words

Trace	Write	Color
flat		FLAT
fly		FLY
fire		FIRE
foot		FOOT
final		FINAL
sofa		SOFA
hoof		HOOF

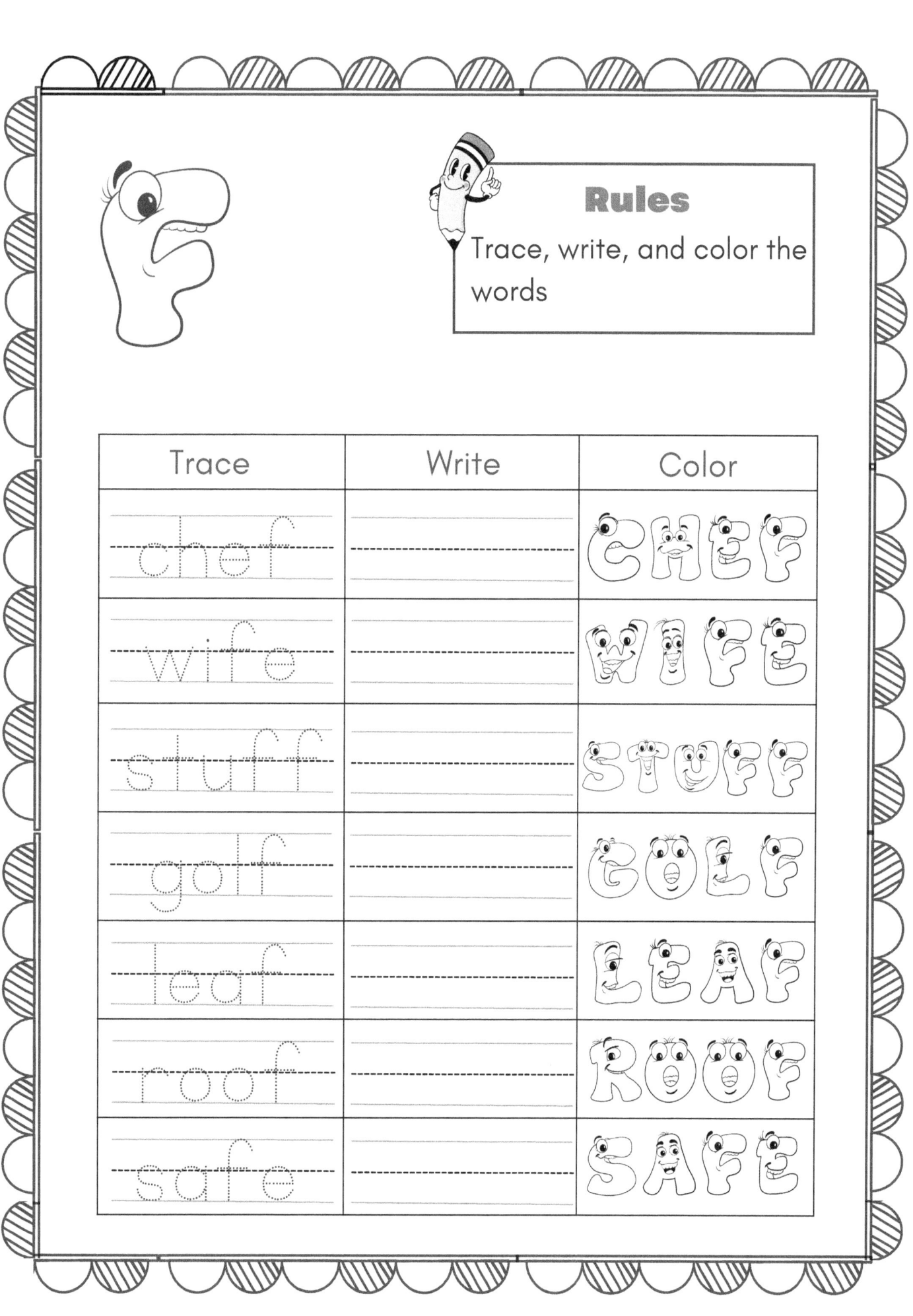

Rules

Trace, write, and color the words

Trace	Write	Color
chef		CHEF
wife		WIFE
stuff		STUFF
golf		GOLF
leaf		LEAF
roof		ROOF
safe		SAFE

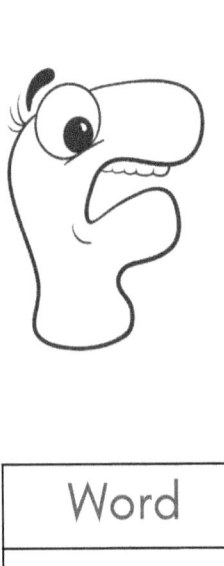

Rules

Read each word and then mark the appropriate box indicating where the letter 'f' is located in the word – at the beginning, middle, or end

Word	Beginning	Middle	End
befit		X	
face	X		
cuff			X
fox			
defer			
farm			
fly			
roof			
safer			
fur			
safe			
beef			

Reading list

Read every word aloud!

food	fun	felt	fig
fat	raft	fly	fed
loft	fact	soft	fee
fan	fad	fop	full
ruff	buff	jeff	staff
tuff	fuzz	fizz	fax
fang	flood	left	flow
fleet	feat	fear	fail
fair	lofty	flour	fowl
for	offer	fits	flag
flood	flood	feed	flip

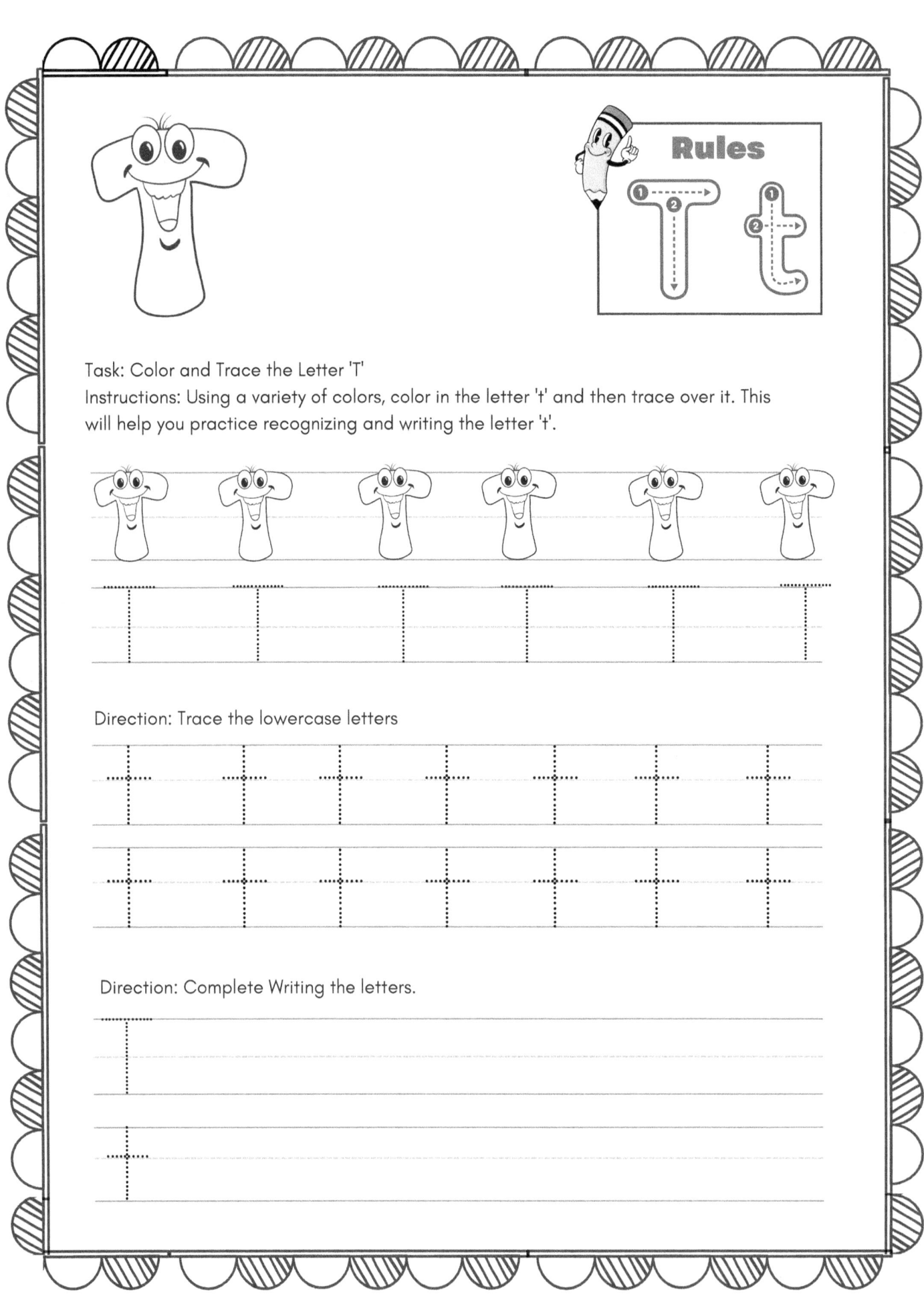

Rules

Task: Color and Trace the Letter 'T'
Instructions: Using a variety of colors, color in the letter 't' and then trace over it. This will help you practice recognizing and writing the letter 't'.

Direction: Trace the lowercase letters

Direction: Complete Writing the letters.

Rules

First, trace the sentence.
Then write it on your own.

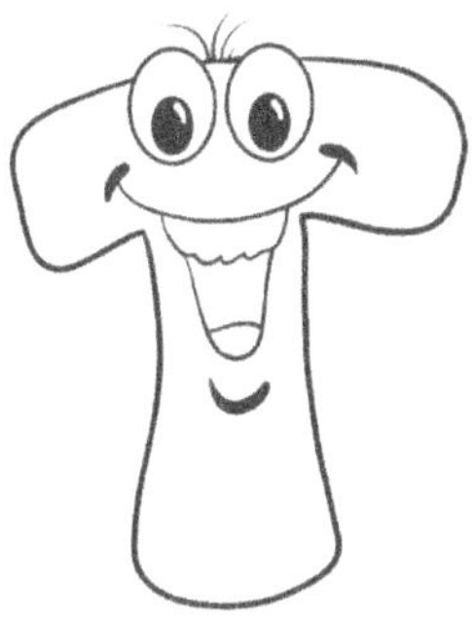

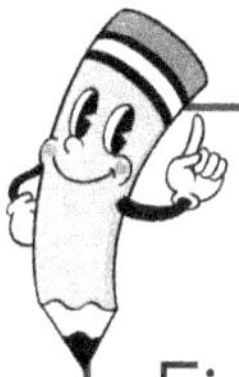

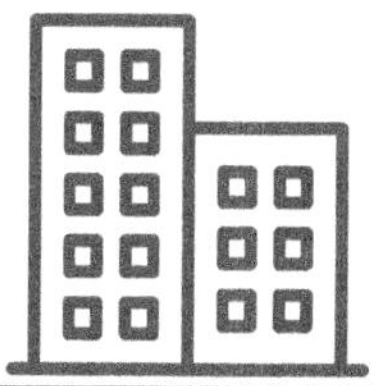

Tall building

Tall

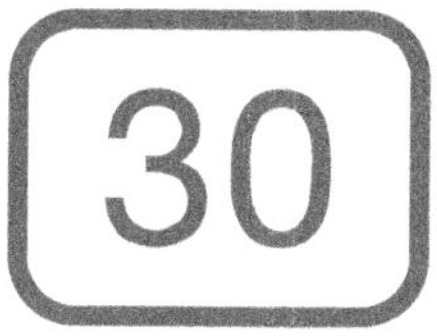

He turned thirty

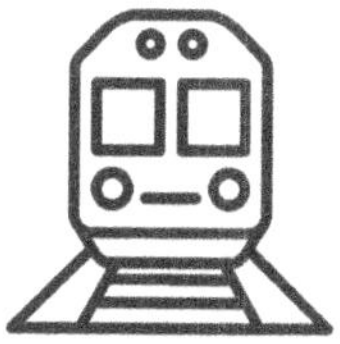

Train ticket

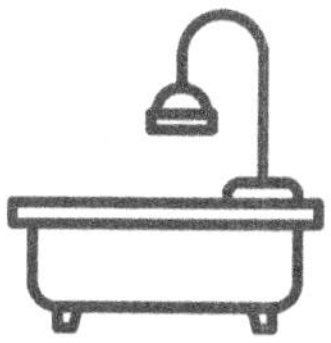

I took a hot bath

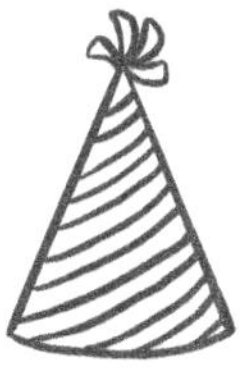

My tenth birthday

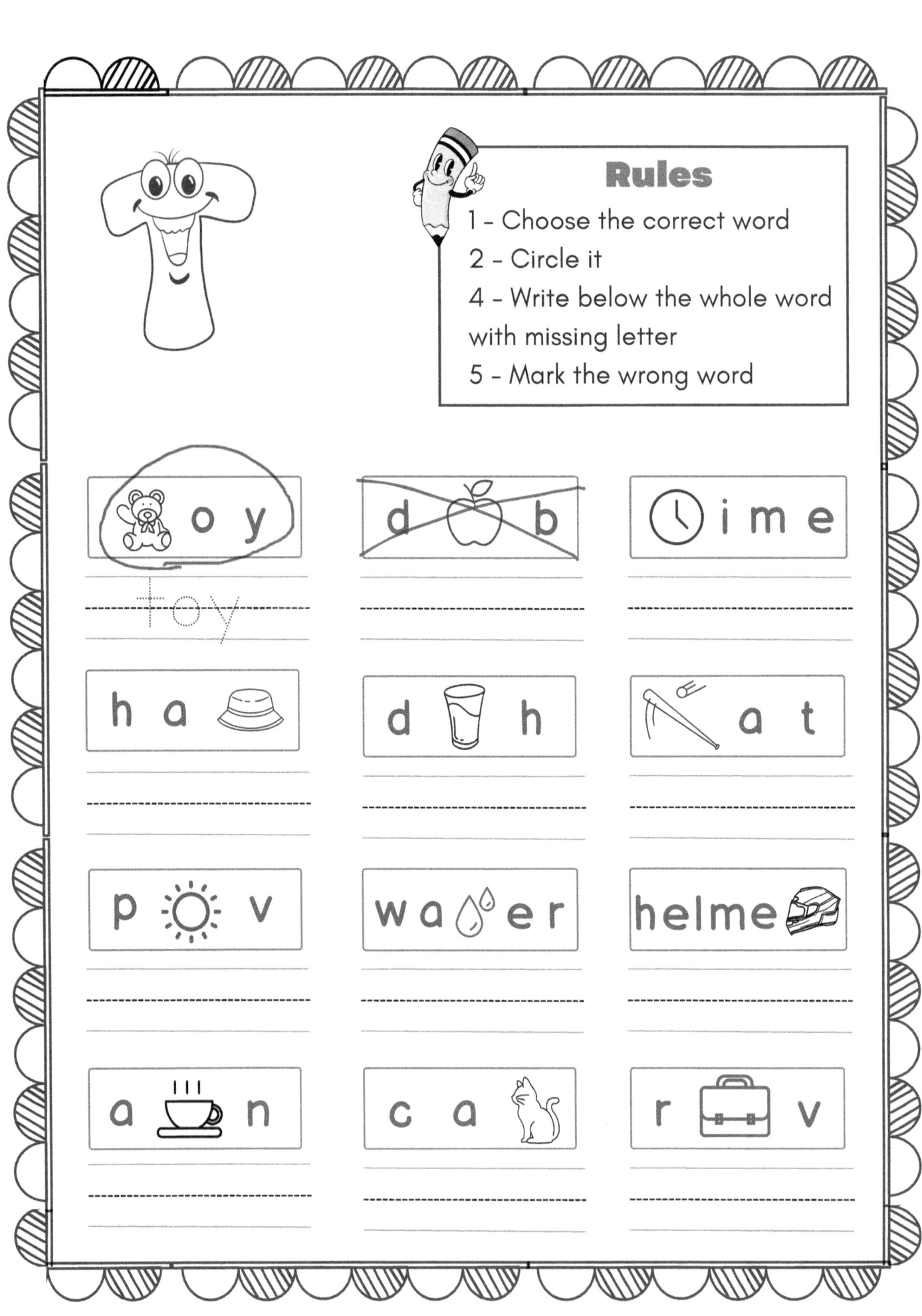

Rules

1 – Choose the correct word
2 – Circle it
4 – Write below the whole word with missing letter
5 – Mark the wrong word

t o y

toy

d ~~🍎~~ b

🕐 i m e

h a 🪣

d 🥛 h

⛏ a t

p ☀ v

wa💧er

helme🪖

a ☕ n

c a 🐱

r 💼 v

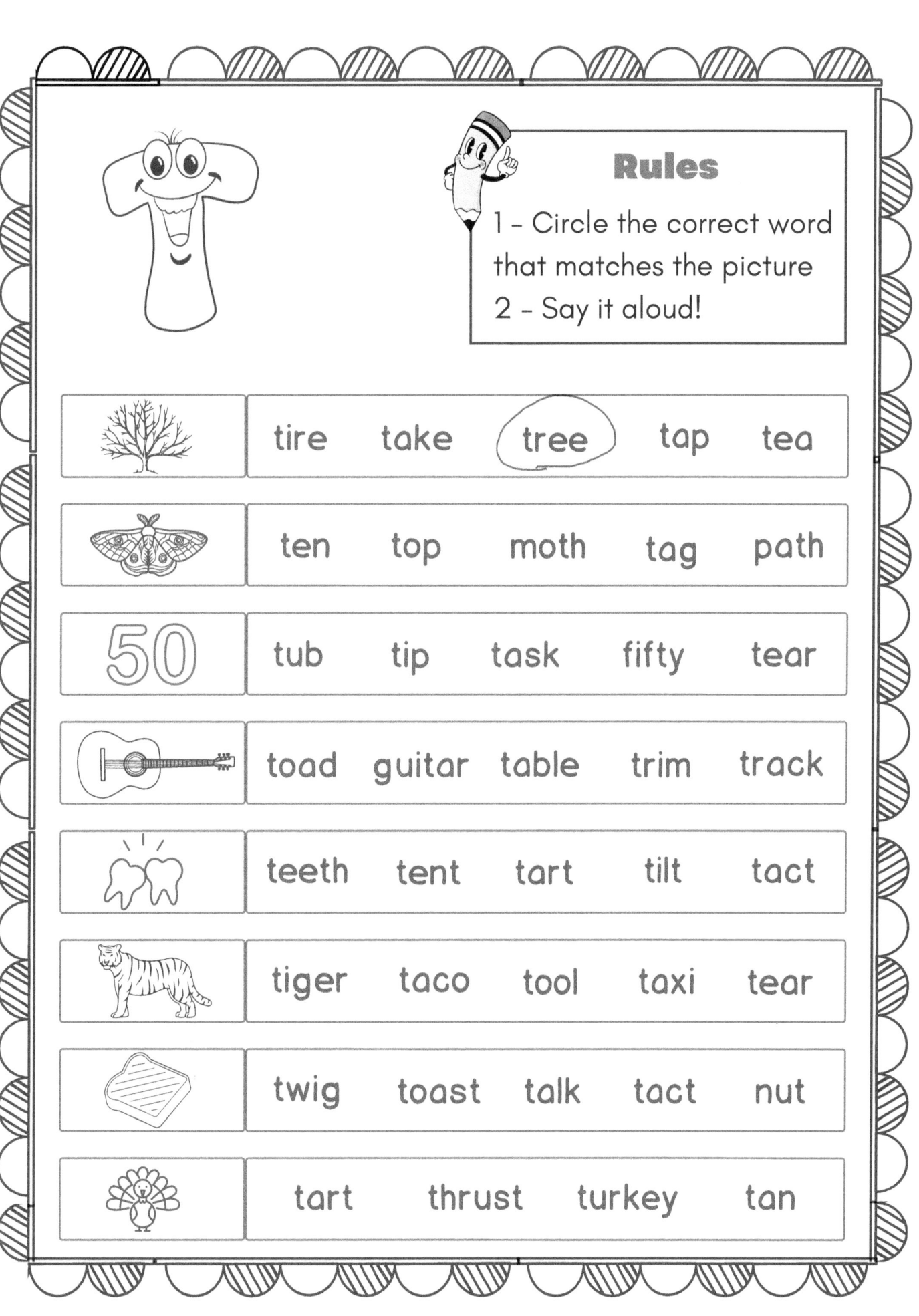

Rules

1 – Circle the correct word that matches the picture
2 – Say it aloud!

	tire take (tree) tap tea
	ten top moth tag path
	tub tip task fifty tear
	toad guitar table trim track
	teeth tent tart tilt tact
	tiger taco tool taxi tear
	twig toast talk tact nut
	tart thrust turkey tan

Rules

Trace, write, and color the words

Trace	Write	Color
hat		HAT
bet		BET
tom		TOM
stud		STUD
tam		TAM
hot		HOT
tim		TIM

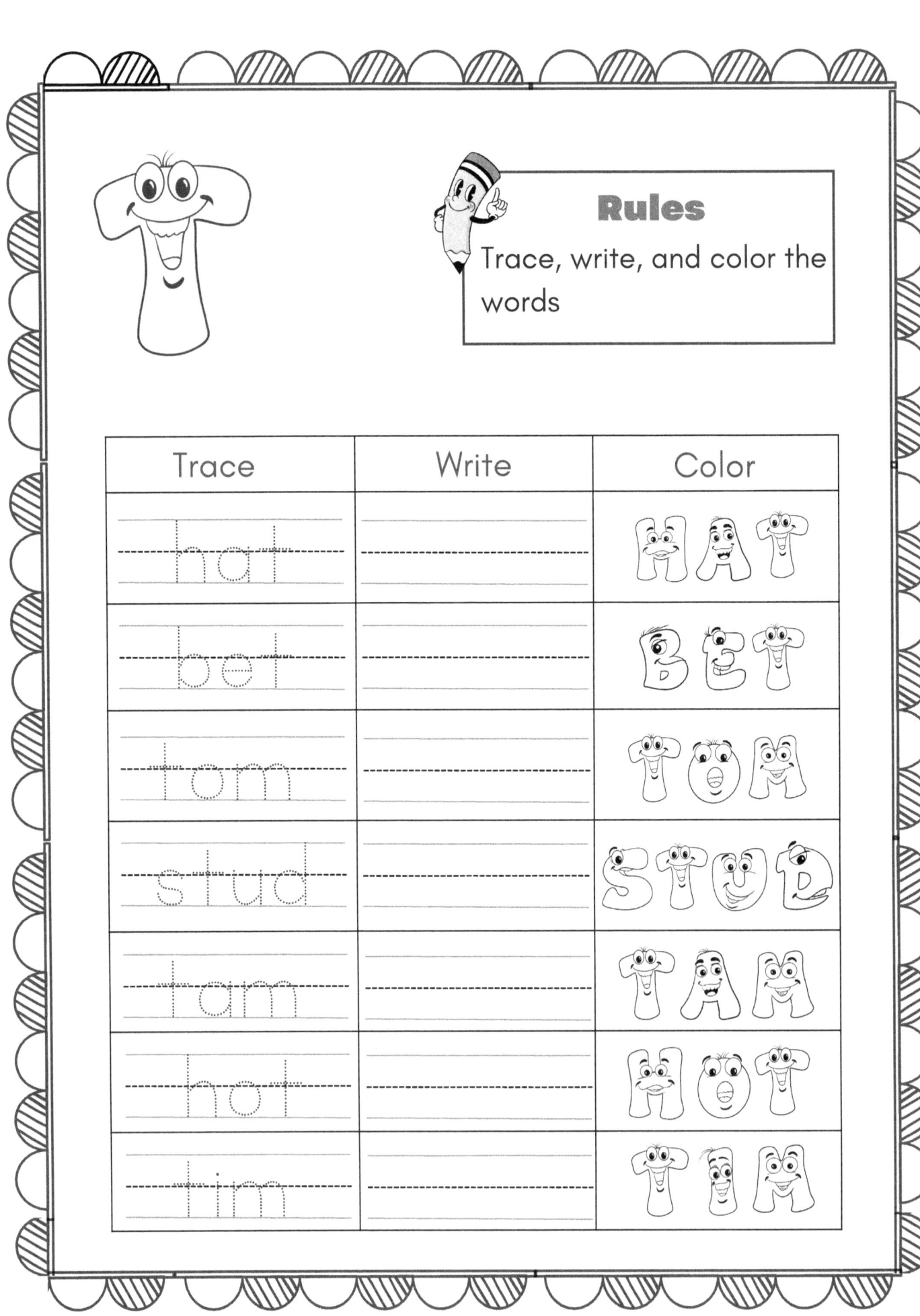

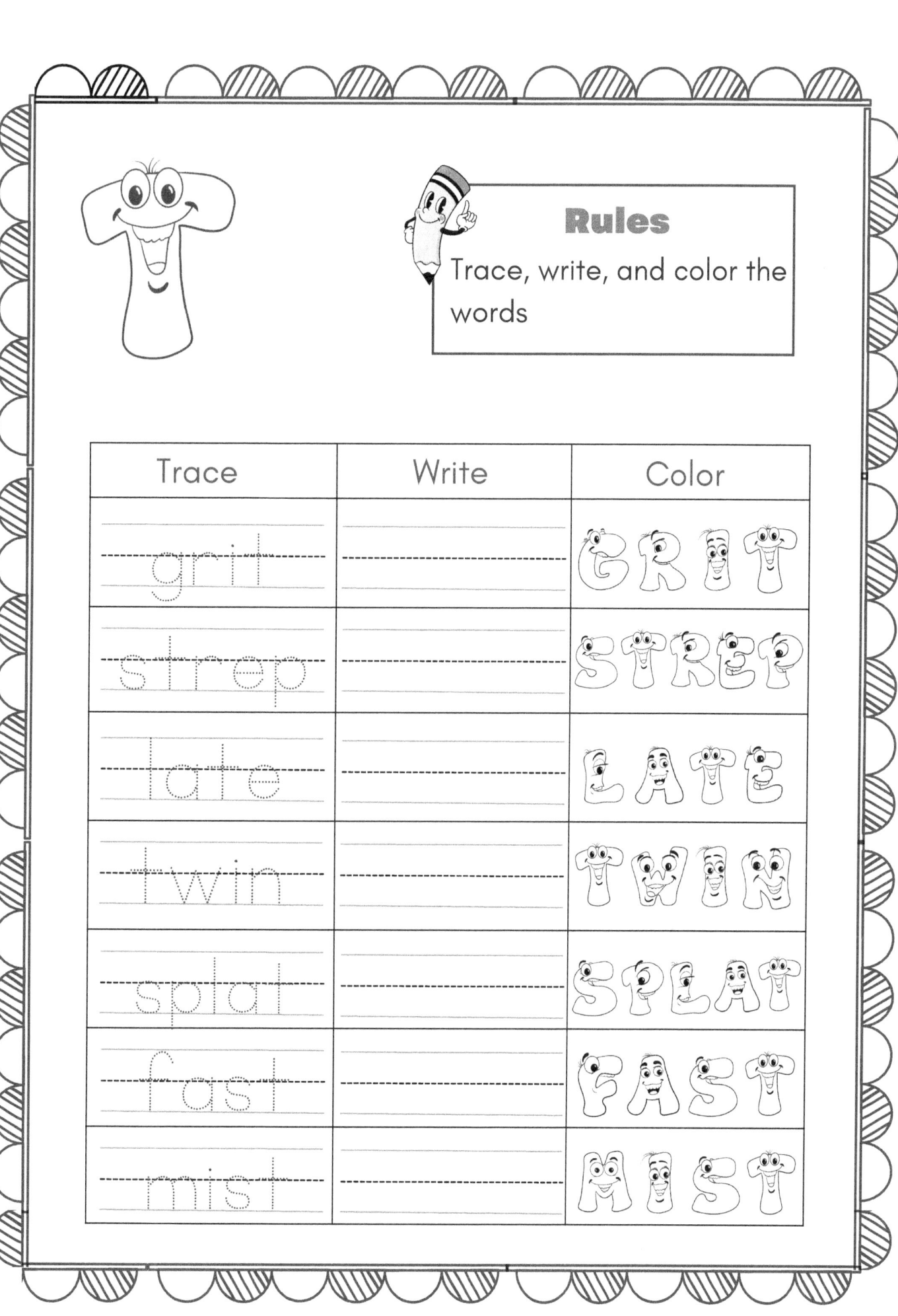

Rules

Trace, write, and color the words

Trace	Write	Color
grit		GRIT
strep		STREP
late		LATE
twin		TWIN
splat		SPLAT
fast		FAST
mist		MIST

Word	Beginning	Middle	End
cast			X
toy	X		
strap		X	
tool			
city			
test			
beauty			
tape			
just			
pant			
potato			
must			

Reading list

Read every word aloud!

tap	ten	top	tub
tag	tug	tin	tar
tee	toad	tale	team
tip	toast	touch	tooth
tidy	tutor	tonic	hint
table	timber	tummy	cat
dent	fruit	bat	turtle
vent	late	right	not
pot	hilt	tassel	team
tingle	tramp	talent	tiny
pant	tint	trite	tangle

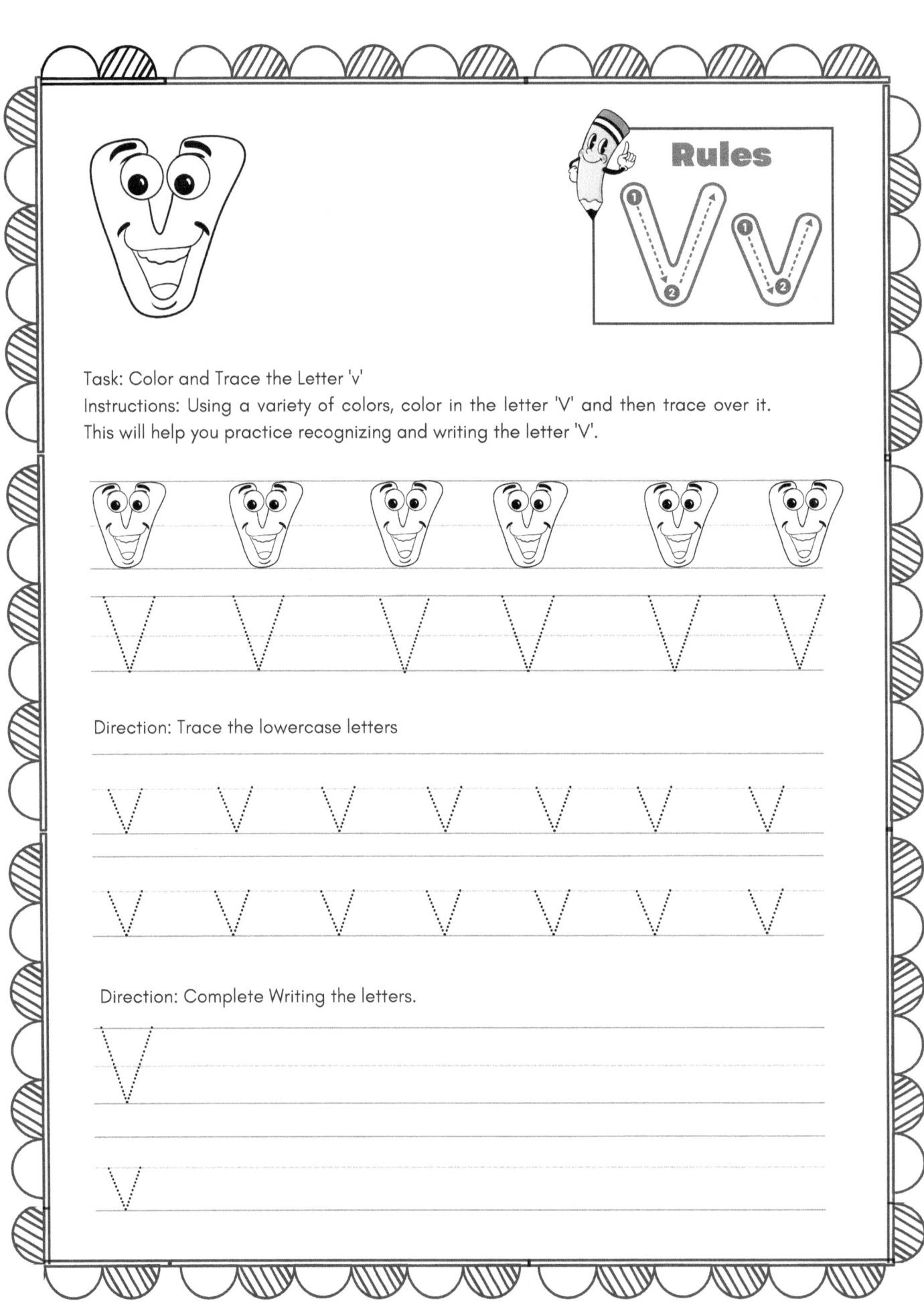

Rules

Task: Color and Trace the Letter 'v'

Instructions: Using a variety of colors, color in the letter 'V' and then trace over it. This will help you practice recognizing and writing the letter 'V'.

Direction: Trace the lowercase letters

Direction: Complete Writing the letters.

Rules

First, trace the sentence.
Then write it on your own.

The bus veered

The

The clever boy

The brave lion

I bought a vase

I have five books

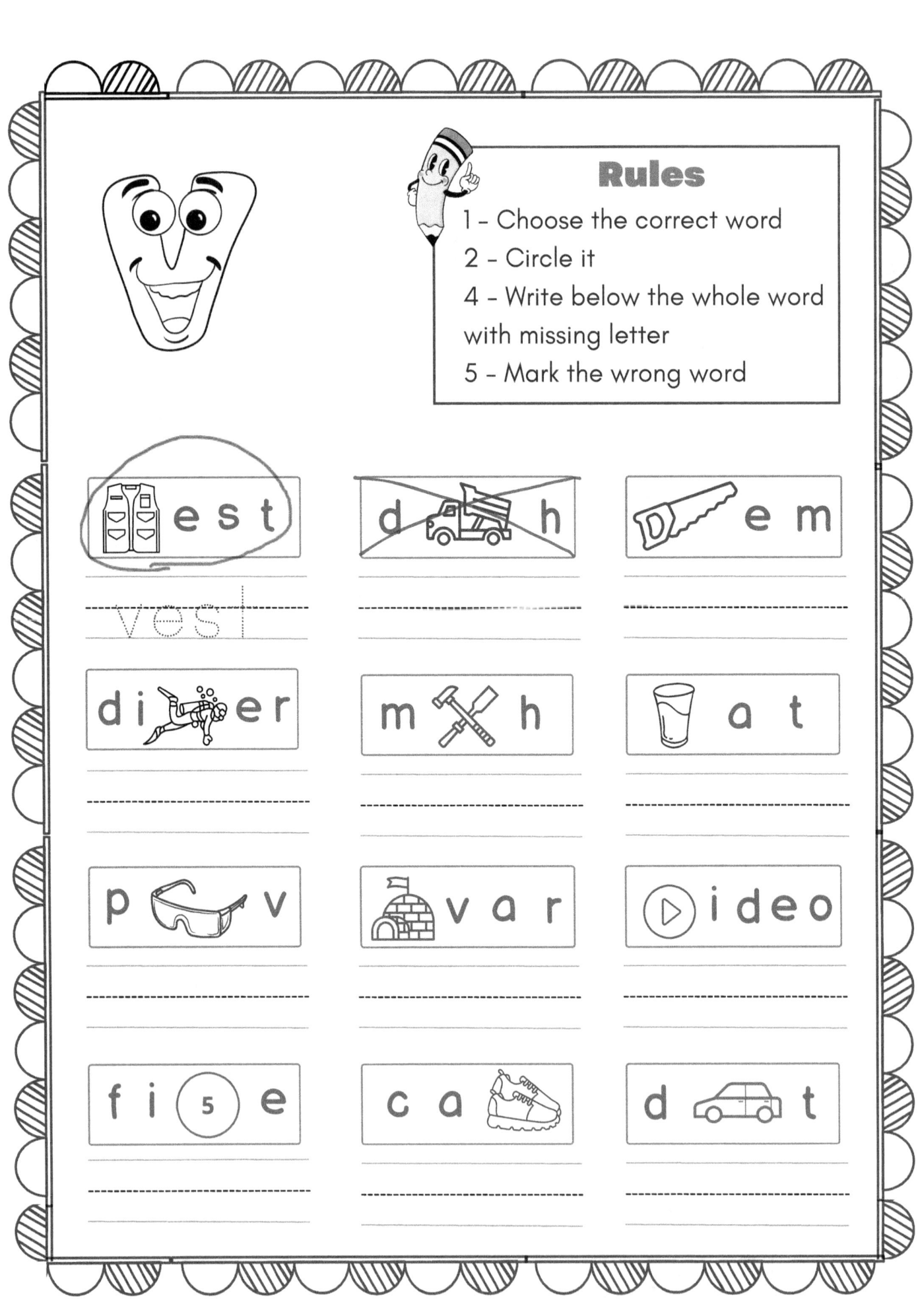

Rules

1 – Choose the correct word

2 – Circle it

4 – Write below the whole word with missing letter

5 – Mark the wrong word

v est

vest

d h

D e m

di v er

m h

a t

p v

v a r

i deo

fi 5 e

c a

d t

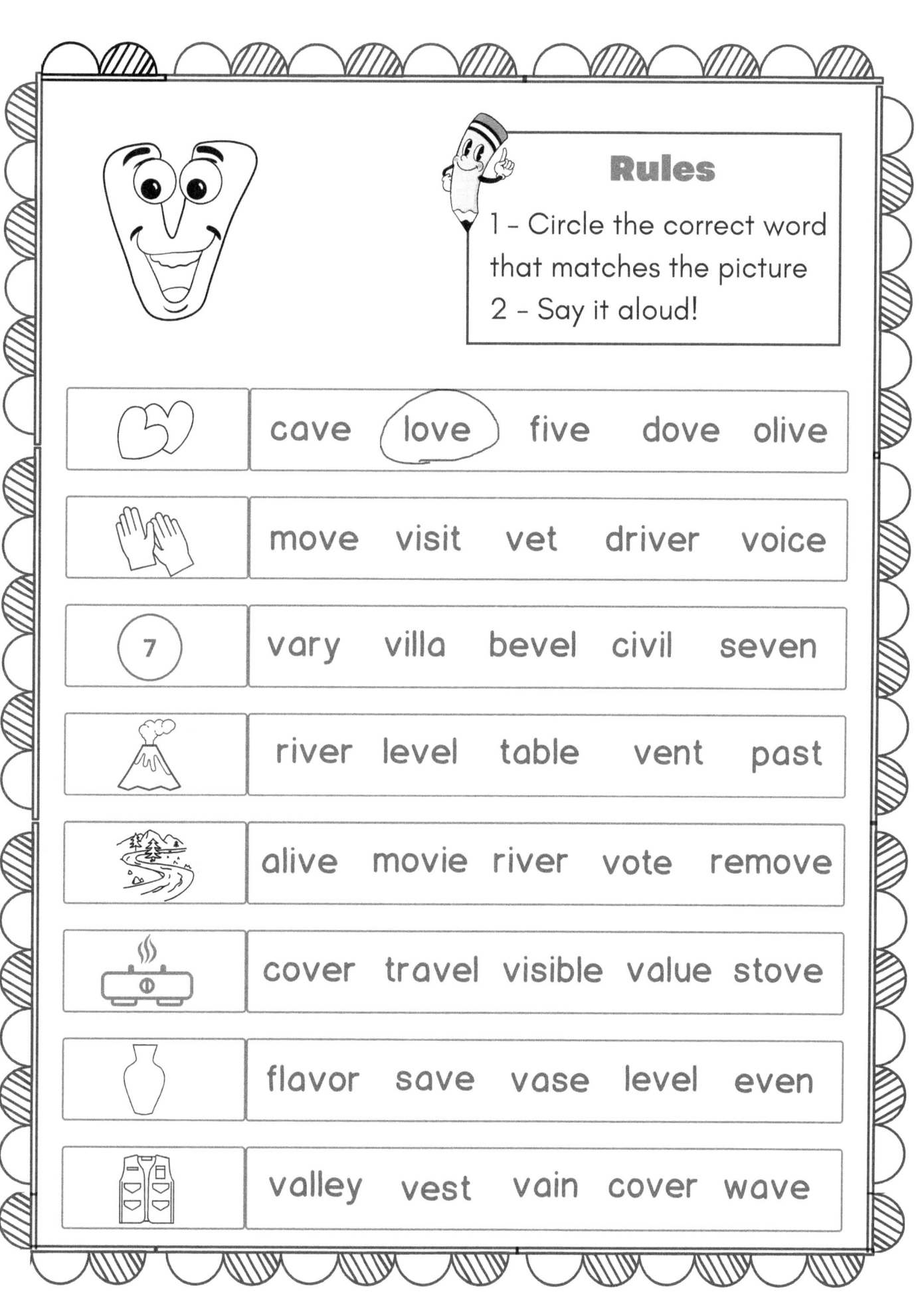

cave (love) five dove olive

move visit vet driver voice

vary villa bevel civil seven

river level table vent past

alive movie river vote remove

cover travel visible value stove

flavor save vase level even

valley vest vain cover wave

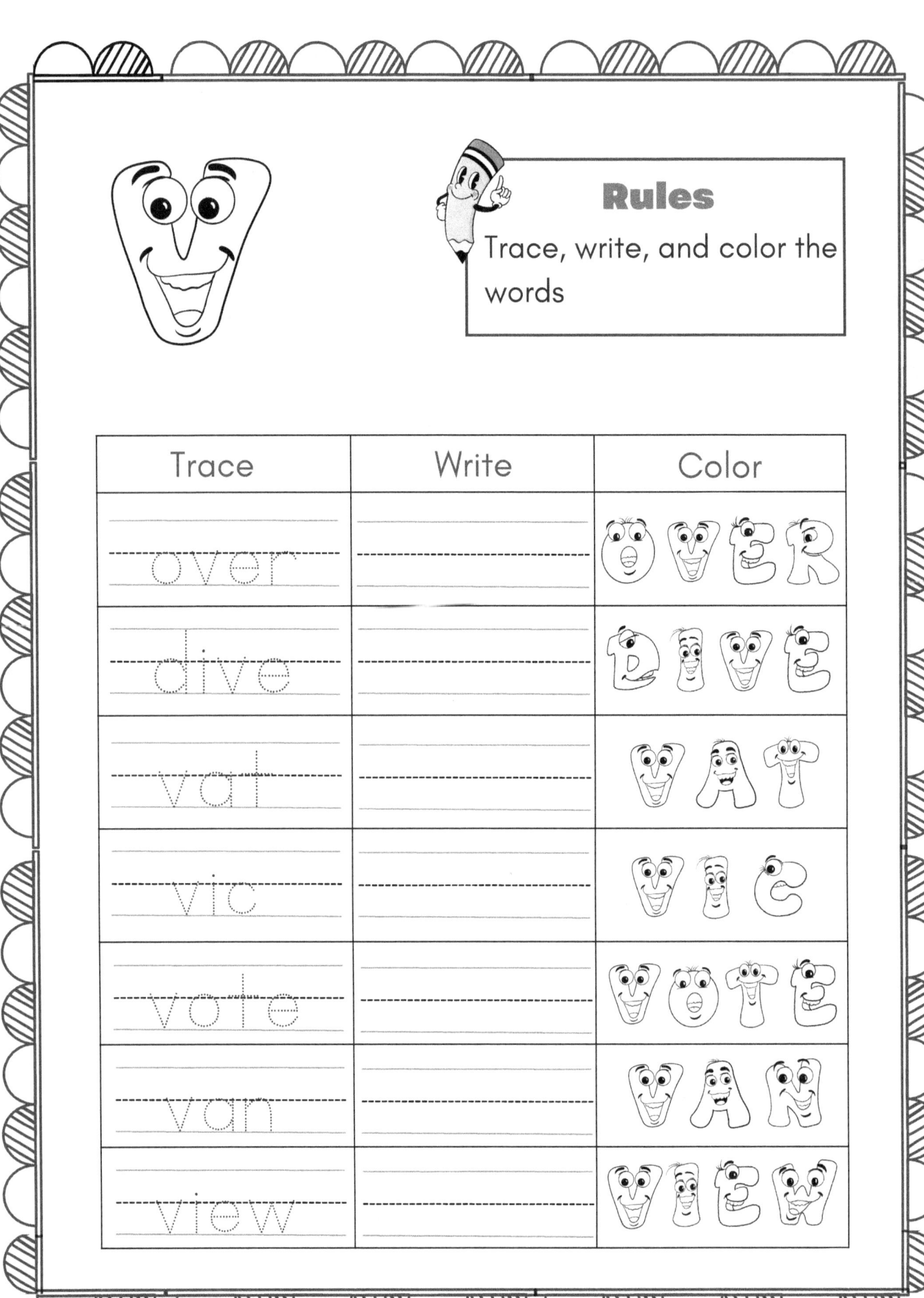

Rules

Trace, write, and color the words

Trace	Write	Color
over		OVER
dive		DIVE
vat		VAT
vic		VIC
vote		VOTE
van		VAN
view		VIEW

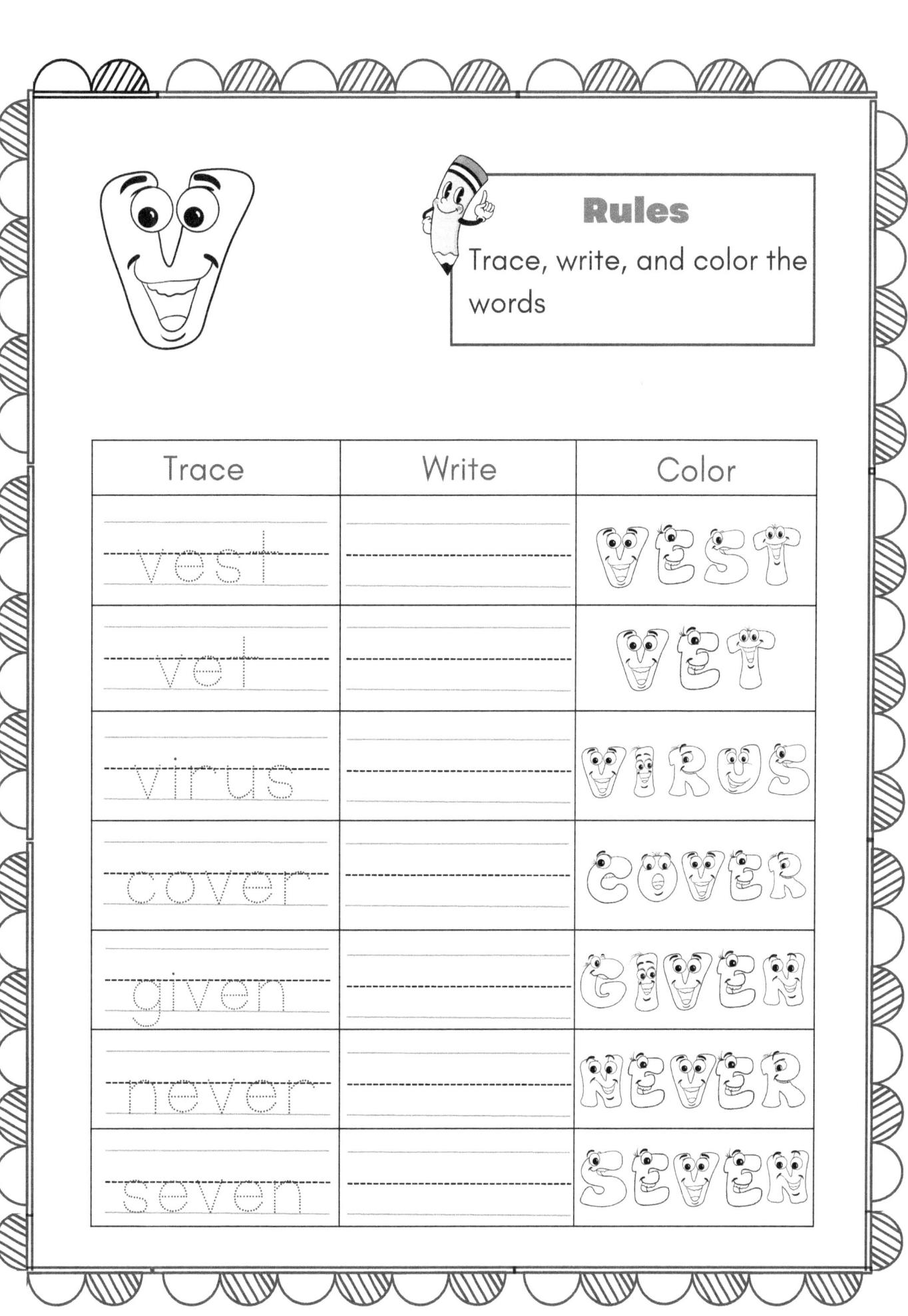

Rules

Trace, write, and color the words

Trace	Write	Color
vest		VEST
vet		VET
virus		VIRUS
cover		COVER
given		GIVEN
never		NEVER
seven		SEVEN

Rules

Read each word and then mark the appropriate box indicating where the letter 'V' is located in the word – at the beginning, middle, or end

Word	Beginning	Middle	End
dev			X
save		X	
vine	X		
give			
vex			
van			
live			
dive			
advice			
elever			
daven			
vote			

Reading list

Read every word aloud!

van	vet	vase	vest
seven	vine	vote	vault
veil	level	leave	viper
solve	volley	ever	velvet
never	vortex	voyage	visit
move	prove	verve	voice
voodoo	cave	brave	save
vent	dive	strive	arrive
vocal	viola	villain	steve
vex	event	veto	volt
value	love	vogue	vary

Thank you

Thank you for choosing our decodable book for struggling readers in grade 1. We understand that reading can be challenging for some children, and our goal is to help them develop the skills they need to become confident readers.

Our book is specifically tailored to meet the needs of struggling readers in grade 1. It focuses on letters and sounds that are commonly confused, such as b, d, p, and q, and includes engaging activities that help children practice these skills. We also included various phonics games, word associations, matching, coloring, and more, to make learning enjoyable and engaging.

We believe that learning to read should be a fun and exciting experience, and that's why we included cheerful illustrations and coloring comic alphabets to help children remember sight words. By making the learning process enjoyable, we hope to instill a lifelong love of reading in your child.

We appreciate your trust in our book and hope that it proves to be a valuable tool in your child's reading journey. We would love to hear your feedback on the book and how it has helped your child. Your opinion matters to us, and it will assist us in creating even more valuable resources for struggling readers in the future.

Thank you again for choosing our decodable book, and we wish you and your child all the best in their reading journey.

Best regards,

[Jed Dolton]